CALLING IN

IN

HOW TO START MAKING
CHANGE WITH THOSE YOU'D
RATHER CANCEL

LORETTA J. ROSS

Simon & Schuster

New York   Amsterdam/Antwerp   Toronto
London   Sydney   New Delhi

Simon & Schuster
1230 Avenue of the Americas
New York, NY 10020

First Simon & Schuster hardcover edition February 2025

SIMON & SCHUSTER and colophon are registered trademarks of
Simon & Schuster, LLC

For information about special discounts for bulk purchases, please contact
Simon & Schuster Special Sales at 1-866-506-1949 or
business@simonandschuster.com.

The Simon & Schuster Speakers Bureau can bring authors to your live event. For
more information or to book an event, contact the Simon & Schuster Speakers
Bureau at 1-866-248-3049 or visit our website at www.simonspeakers.com.

Interior design by Wendy Blum

Manufactured in the United States of America

1   3   5   7   9   10   8   6   4   2

Library of Congress Cataloging-in-Publication Data has been applied for.

ISBN 978-1-9821-9079-8
ISBN 978-1-9821-9081-1 (ebook)

CONTENTS

CALLING IN

PROLOGUE

In the course of history, there comes a time when humanity is called to shift to a new level of consciousness. To reach a higher moral ground. A time when we have to shed our fear and give hope to each other.

—Wangari Maathai, Nobel lecture, 2014

I'm a reformed call out queen. I've furiously called out enemies. I've righteously called out friends. I've gleefully called out strangers. I even once called out President Barack Obama, although that's a story for another time. My ego sure gets the appeal of putting people on blast. But I also realized a long time ago that running my mouth never did seem to accomplish what I wanted it to.

I have been a human rights activist since the early 1970s. I've been the voice who picks up the phone to help rape victims in the most humiliating times of their lives—times they'd rather forget. I've been an opposition researcher, attending Klan rallies and working to deprogram white supremacists who've spent their lives devoted to hate. I've been a bridge between warring factions of feminists and progressives, finding new conversations that can unite us, pursuing common goals instead of prying us apart.

In the past five decades, I've learned a lot about what works to create change. And I've learned a lot about what *doesn't*—often, the hard way. I've been proud to watch the human rights values I've espoused take hold in our culture, turning ideas that once seemed radical into mainstream beliefs. I've been proud to watch movements like Black Lives Matter, Reproductive Justice, and #MeToo spread far and wide, and to witness how new generations have joined the fight for justice, demanding action on global warming, insisting that health care and affordable housing are human rights, and asserting that a college education should not be a ticket to lifelong debt.

Those most likely to have their human rights violated are typically the ones who believe the most in the promise of human rights, while our critics and skeptics tend to be those whose human rights are most protected by the status quo. Opponents mockingly call us SJWs— social justice warriors—but we're really human rights activists with a forward-facing global vision for the twenty-first century. Opponents fear us because their idealized society is fixated on centuries past when violence against political opponents was normal and when we stayed in our place. If another world is possible, then another America is necessary. I'm so inspired by how many people are doing the work to bring it about.

But, in the past decade, I've also seen a spike of infighting, cruelty, and call outs among could-be allies. This has always been a danger among radical movements: it's what hamstrung the groups I worked with in DC in the 1970s when I started my journey as a social justice activist. I now often talk to people who are clear-eyed and adamant about their values and yet who feel unbearably drained by the toxic atmosphere in which they're working. Or I speak with well-meaning people who want to help but are afraid to lend their efforts—because they don't know the right language or where to begin without being reamed out.

This isn't how it should be—nor how it has to be.

The terms "cancel culture" and "call out culture" have become a political Rorschach test. Since Trump's first run for president, the Right has bemoaned cancel culture, even as they seek to ban more books, more history, more art, and more ways of living than anyone on the Left. They don't want to teach an honest history of America because they want to repeat the sins of the past. They carp about wokeness, pronouns, and feminism, while they lack any discernible agenda for addressing the country's problems. Stroking the outrage culture is their priority. And call outs are an easy target for their rage.

Progressives, meanwhile, have responded reactively, defending call outs as mere "consequences" or "accountability" measures for bad actors. Sometimes this is true. But cancel culture can also be weaponized, by the Right or the Left. Offenses—someone's not woke enough, someone's not patriotic enough—can get treated as five-alarm fires, until we've reached a point where it becomes difficult to critique cancel culture without risking being canceled ourselves.

I know the allure of calling people out all too well. I've scorched others with righteous anger, and I've been burned by my ego. I have to trap words in my brain before they come out of my mouth a dozen times a day. Because I know it's better if I do. I've seen families torn apart over political differences because they don't know how to love each other despite their disagreements. I've been part of movements that have disintegrated due to their inability to distinguish between allies and enemies. I've seen how a moment of opportunity can slip away while we're caught up in morality plays or power fights.

And I see the warning signs right now, for progressives and our country as a whole. Bitter partisanship has caused many of us to hate fellow Americans. It's made people afraid to build community. It's divided families. Almost everyone is anxious for fear of saying the wrong thing. People are distancing themselves and suffering emotionally. Powerless to do anything about geopolitical conflicts, we turn on family and friends.

Anyone who thinks this is okay doesn't care about our country and doesn't care about honesty, integrity, or mercy. These are, perhaps, old-fashioned terms, but they matter to me and they should matter to all of us. I have no interest in respectability politics—no interest in being polite and uncontroversial in the hope of gaining others' approval. But I *am* interested in living out my values.

I get why it can be easy to forget all this. We are sensitive to our despair and the despair of others. We are all struggling to make sense of everything that is going on. We refuse to accept the status quo that judges us because of our skin color, sexual orientation, gender identity, class, citizenship, abilities, political affiliation, or any other infuriating, irrelevant reason. We witness our loved ones pulling in a different direction in ways that often don't make sense to us. We yearn to be part of something bigger than ourselves, something that gives our life meaning. But it is not enough to be correct; we must take correct action.

People opposed to human rights—opposed to ending poverty, addressing racism, or accepting women's rights to control their bodies—think they're fighting the human rights movement, but I believe they're wrong. They're fighting truth, history, and evidence. Most importantly, they're fighting time. These existential forces are beyond their power to command. With truth, history, evidence, and time on our side, we hold the winning hand despite our fears of powerlessness and failure. Our opponents are simply pimples on the ass of time. But my biggest fear is that despite our winning hand, we'll be defeated—at least in our lifetimes—because we can't stop calling one another out.

I've learned that there *is* a better way. We can skip the viral shaming and reputational warfare. We can skip the ideological litmus tests that don't help to build a diverse coalition. Whether persuading another individual or launching an entire cultural movement, real change requires bringing people *in*. Even people you expected not to need or not to be able to reach.

This is why I've come to embrace Calling In.

Calling in considers whether we can connect with others before we start shouting them down. It allows us to reach other people as *people*, to breathe a little easier, and, ultimately, to get things done. Calling in builds bridges instead of burning them down so that we might walk together along the path toward collective liberation.

The difference is tactical—and so I'll suggest new words, methods, and attitudes throughout this book—but it's also philosophical. Calling in can help us model the world we want to achieve at the end of our efforts: a world with more joy and forgiveness and less shame and cruelty, a world where people don't need to feel afraid and can feel empowered to pursue the common good, even if we make mistakes along the way. We can avoid the shame of not *being* enough, or not *knowing* enough.

For more than forty years now, I've oriented my philosophy for enacting change and building movements around calling in. In the first four chapters of this book, I'll explore the theory behind this approach and show you how it gets results. I'll also diagnose where call out culture came from, why it's become a cultural monster—especially on social media—and why no one seems to be able to talk about it without losing their head. Then, in the last four chapters, I'll show you the techniques you'll need to put the principles of calling in into action.

Most of us respond emotionally to call outs without recognizing their patterns and intentions. We need to think more systematically. We need to create strategies for engaging with disagreements, so we're prepared in advance. I've created what I call the "5Cs"—a spectrum of accountability measures to help us figure out how to respond depending on the situation, whether by *calling out* (yes, I think call outs do have their uses, as I'll discuss in chapter 2), *canceling, calling in, calling on* (asking people to do better, but without investing your time and energy in helping them to change), or *calling it off*. When it's not possible to call in people with love and respect, we can choose another option that better suits where we are emotionally at the time. There's no shame in deciding to call it off. As I'll discuss in chapters 5 and 7, I think it's essential to recognize when saying nothing is the healthiest tactic for you in the moment.

We can recognize the patterns of call outs and understand our options for deploying these techniques, and we'll realize we're more knowledgeable about how to have challenging conversations than we think. Together, over time, we can transform our culture that excludes and impugns people into a culture that invites people in.

I'm not alone in thinking this. In this book, I've combined stories and lessons from my life as an activist with the wisdom of many younger thinkers, including Ngọc Loan Trần (who coined the term "Calling In"), Mariame Kaba, Kelly Hayes, and especially adrienne maree brown, who constantly awes me with her grace and brilliance. I also reference our iconic guiding lights like Audre Lorde, James Baldwin, and Martin Luther King Jr. I've woven in insights from experts in psychology, philosophy, history, and other disciplines that probe how people experience and respond to criticism. I've also included perspectives from analysts on the right and center of US politics, and from many people who exist somewhere in between the labels we use.

Of course, I don't agree with everything someone who I cite has ever said, but I find that to be an unnecessarily high bar; my life has taught me many lessons from the most unlikely people when I dared to listen.

I believe the practical advice in these pages is essential for anyone who wants to be part of a vibrant human rights movement. But it's important for less politically active people too. These are techniques that any leader or activist, any friend or partner, any family member or acquaintance can learn to practice to be kinder to one another.

I'm so excited to share them with you. But first, let me show you how I got here—how calling in entered my life.

1.

HOW I LEARNED TO CALL IN

I know the world is bruised and bleeding, and though it is important not to ignore its pain, it is also critical to refuse to succumb to its malevolence.

—Toni Morrison

When the iron gate slammed shut behind me, I shuffled forward and held out my arms. The two male prison guards reached out and touched too much, fondling me as they searched for contraband. They seemed to relish it. I tried to block them out, to retreat into a little corner in my mind. I didn't even want to breathe until it was over.

A gruff voice, a buzz, then another set of bars swung open, and I stepped through. When the last gate clanged, I was surrounded by stark concrete walls.

I was locked in now, about to encounter a man who was someone's nightmare. Who might yet be mine?

Lorton Reformatory housed the men who'd been convicted of the worst crimes in the nation's capital. It was 1979 and I was twenty-six.

I was the newly minted director of the Washington, DC Rape Crisis Center, and I had driven an hour to the notorious Northern Virginia prison on an unusual mission. I had come to talk to a man who was serving a life sentence for raping and murdering a woman. I had come to talk to him about why *not* to rape. One-on-one, face-to-face.

On the way in, the prison had looked like an idyllic college campus—vibrant green quads, trim brick buildings, perfect archways, and curved walkways—until you saw the watchtower, armed with guards and rifles, and barbed wire. Until you'd felt the guards' touch. Until you heard the *clang*.

But now—*What the f*!# am I doing here?* I felt scared and unprepared. I had no particular qualifications for this visit, and I could no longer tell you what I'd been thinking when I'd agreed to it.

The man I'd arranged to see was named William Fuller. He had written to the Center months earlier, asking for help. I can still remember the crux of his letter, more than forty years later: "Outside I raped women; inside I rape men. I'd like not to be a rapist anymore." He was serving a life sentence for raping and murdering a Black schoolteacher named Ethel Dorsey. He had been incarcerated for fifteen years by that time.

Fuller's letter sparked passionate disagreement at the Center. Our organization had been around since 1972, when it launched as the first rape crisis center in the country. But it still ran understaffed on a threadbare budget. Most of us were offended by the letter. We didn't have enough resources to help *victims*. How dare a rapist seek help from us? Some employees thought the letter was a setup; maybe Fuller was trying to manipulate us into becoming mules to smuggle contraband. Others thought it might be a ploy to drum up illicit conjugal visits. Or perhaps it was a long play, to get the Center to support a parole application.

My first response was outright anger, followed closely by disgust. I wanted to send this man my own outraged letter, calling him out for even *thinking* we would talk to him. Once I'd read his note, I didn't want to touch it, as if the paper itself was contaminated.

Yet I couldn't put the letter out of my mind. And, tellingly, I hadn't thrown it into the trash. The letter sat on my desk for months, lurking beneath other paperwork but never forgotten. It was like a loose tooth I couldn't stop wiggling.

Eventually, my curiosity won. Over the objections of some of the other staffers, I wrote back, offering a counseling session. We had never worked with perpetrators before, only rape victims. We offered all manner of support, and it was important work, but something was frustrating me. Our work wasn't stopping any rapists from raping. And I wanted to understand the mind of a rapist, a man from my Black community who chose to brutalize women like me.

It was only as I stood frozen—in that cramped, drab hallway in Lorton Reformatory—that I realized how poorly this could go. I had no plan, no script. And I had no special qualifications, except for one thing: I was a survivor of sexual assault. Those scars were still bleeding all over my life.

What in the world could a rape survivor say to a convicted rapist? What would *I* say, when I walked through the door at the end of the hall and faced him?

Most rape victims don't intentionally resummon their worst memories each day as part of their work. I loved my job at the Rape Crisis Center, but it was a constant reminder of what I'd been through. And, if I'm honest, I had not healed from the pain.

When I was fourteen and entering the tenth grade in the tumultuous summer of 1968, I was molested by a twenty-seven-year-old married cousin, Melvin. Instead of babysitting me while I stayed with our great-aunt, he plied me with alcohol to manipulate my consent to sex. I had never drunk alcohol before, and I felt like he was treating me like a grown woman. I now know this is how many sexual predators groom young girls. What's worse, Melvin apparently thought what he was doing was okay because I'd told him the secret that I was most ashamed of: that I technically wasn't a virgin, that I'd already been raped.

Three years earlier, at age eleven, I'd been kidnapped from a Girl Scout outing at an amusement park. I had wandered away from the troop after chasing a place in line for a coveted ride. As I roamed around the edges of the park seeking my mom and the other girls, a uniformed young GI from the local army base offered to help. My father was a retired army veteran, having served in three wars. I'd been surrounded by GIs all my life and thought I could trust him. Instead, he drove me into the nearby woods and raped me, repeatedly punching me in the face because I wouldn't stop screaming. I retreated into my mind; I didn't know what was happening. Strangely, the kidnapper asked where I lived after the assault, and returned me to my neighborhood. He could have left my bloody body in the woods, but perversely, he acted as if we'd simply been on a date, kissing me goodbye when he dropped me off.

The only person at home was my older sister, Carol. Upon seeing my battered face and bloody white jeans, Carol helped me wash up and put me to bed. Since she was nine years older than me, I'm sure she knew what happened, even if I couldn't tell her. I didn't have the words. I don't know what she told Mom, but I know that Mom never asked why I didn't come home with the other girls. This was when I learned that we were a family who kept our secrets deeply buried. I didn't tell my parents because I was afraid I'd be in trouble. At the time, I thought the rape was my punishment from God for getting into a car with a stranger.

They say a parent is only as happy as their least happy child. I was Mom's unhappy child after that. Three summers later, she sent me to stay with my great-aunt, perhaps to get some space in our tumultuous relationship. Or maybe to get a break from my brooding unhappiness that we couldn't talk about. The silence of misery wore us down. That's how Melvin found me—lonely and miserable.

After I told my cousin Melvin he'd gotten me pregnant, he accused me of trying to entrap him and break up his marriage. I was fourteen. I had hoped he would have a magical solution for me, a way to end the pregnancy, although my knowledge of abortion was nonexistent. I just needed his help. But he fled, afraid of what my father might do. He hastily joined the merchant marines and left the country, abandoning me, his wife, and his three children.

I feared my parents would blame me because I blamed myself, so I hid the pregnancy as long as I could. I went to bed every night praying it was a nightmare that would be over when I woke. When I finally disclosed the pregnancy in my fifth month, my horrified parents sent me to a secret home for unwed mothers. They believed that abortion was not an accessible or safe option for me in 1968, and it was a widespread practice back then to hide teen pregnancies if families could afford to send their daughters away. I could pretend to have been on an extended vacation like the rest of the twenty girls sequestered at the Salvation Army compound near Trinity University in San Antonio. My parents and I planned to give the child up for adoption. I didn't want to become a mother through incest. I'd received early entry and a potential scholarship to Radcliffe College as a National Merit qualifying scholar. I was determined to go to college and not let my rapist's dirty fingerprints determine my destiny.

I was the only Black girl at the compound hidden behind tall, barbed wire fences. The authorities forbade visits from loved ones, so each day was desperately lonely. There was no teenage chatter or gossip. We didn't share how we became pregnant or talk about how our bodies were rapidly changing. We were trapped in a bubble of denial. We lived like we were in a religious order under vows of penitent silence. We slept in a large, sterile dormitory room with no privacy and no visits from doctors, beyond the initial examinations to estimate our expected due dates.

No one told us anything about what to expect or tried to alleviate our anxieties. We endured endless early-morning prayers and cleaning chores. But mostly, we waited to birth these inconvenient "things." We were promised we could be good kids again if we just followed orders.

On April 9, 1969, my son was born at 4:00 a.m., after eighteen tortuous hours of labor that I didn't understand. I remember screaming at each contraction until the delivery doctor demanded I be anesthetized. I was fully unconscious when the baby was born. I later learned this is called a "twilight" birth, a practice now frowned upon.

The next day, the staff at the hospital broke the rules by bringing my son first to me instead of directly to the adoption agency. When they placed him in my arms, all I could say through the after-birth pain was "He's got my face, he's got my face, he's got my face!"

I impulsively axed the adoption plans. My emotions were overwhelming. Mom had refused to come to the hospital during the eighteen-hour delivery, but she rushed there to try to convince me to follow through with the adoption. I've spent years wondering if my refusal was due more to motherly love or adolescent rebellion. My parents hadn't pressured me to consent to the adoption; we all agreed it was the best choice given my future plans. I still don't know why I immediately bonded with that child of incest. All I knew was that we belonged together.

Because I had not thought beyond the pregnancy, I hadn't selected a name for my son's birth certificate. I chose the middle names of two of my five brothers, and I brought Howard Michael Ross home to the bedroom I shared with my severely disabled sister, Toni. Toni, who was only thirteen months younger than me, was bedridden from polio, spinal meningitis, epilepsy, muscular dystrophy, and what was then called "mental retardation." Apparently, she had no immune system when she was born and started contracting all these diseases when she was six months old. She couldn't walk without her braces or feed herself without choking. I was glad not to be still sharing a bed with her because of her permanent incontinence. Having a child meant a separate twin bed, with my baby sleeping with me because the room was too small for a crib too.

By keeping my son, I became a teen mother, a statistic, predicted for failure in a judgmental society that always seemed to blame the girls, never our abusers. My rebellious decision also tethered me to my rapist cousin forever, although I never saw him again.

Of course, everything changed when I tried to return to normal life. I felt radioactive. Instead of walking down hallways swirling with rumors that I'd been pregnant, I went back to school parenting an actual child. I had been one of three Black honors students in a predominantly white high school. I'd gotten straight A's and was in the science club. But when I first tried to return to school, the administrators rejected me, only relenting when my parents threatened to sue for discrimination. Next, the white guidance counselor who had recommended me for early admission to Radcliffe retracted her recommendation, which canceled my scholarship. Luckily, I was able to draw other offers. When I graduated at sixteen, I accepted a scholarship from Howard University, which brought me to DC in 1970.

My parents initially agreed to raise my son while I went off to college, but after my sophomore year, my mother sued for custody. She seemed furious with me in those years, to a degree that I wouldn't be able to comprehend until later. Mom had already raised eight kids, and my son involuntarily extended her parenting just when she thought she was finally finished. I rushed home to collect Howard and then headed back to school, trying to split classes with full-time work while raising my son. My grades suffered, and I lost my scholarship. After my junior year, I couldn't keep the work/life balance necessary to earn a chemistry degree, nor could I afford tuition any longer, so I dropped out. I got a low-paying job at a research laboratory sterilizing glassware and then doubled my salary by falling back on the typing skills I'd learned in middle school, becoming a secretary at a public-interest research firm. I later accepted a job at the National Football League Players Association as their first Black employee.

Two years later, when my apartment building received a ninety-day eviction notice, I stumbled into local political organizing through the tenants' rights movement. And this introduced me to an organizer and former Black Panther Party member named Nkenge Touré. She was the director of the DC Rape Crisis Center, and she invited me to become a volunteer.

Working at the Rape Crisis Center helped save my life and heal my soul. When I joined, I was suicidal, fearful of men yet in a relationship with one, and trying to hold on to my sanity by channeling my rage into political work. I wanted to help other victims, but I was still in total chaos. I hadn't sought therapy yet for my unhealed trauma, so I was self-medicating through drug abuse, hoping no one would peep behind the façade and discover how much of a fraud I felt inside.

At the Center, I started as a volunteer for the 333-RAPE hotline, which meant staying in the office all night to answer the phone. We would receive calls from women who'd been assaulted and try to be there for them emotionally—giving them a shoulder to cry on—and practically, explaining how to hold on to evidence or press charges. We worked in the basement of All Souls Church on Sixteenth Street and generally did nighttime shifts in pairs as a security measure, so no one exited the building alone. It was easy to grow close with the other volunteers and employees. Over time, we conducted informal consciousness-raising sessions, where we spoke with one another about what we had been through. We all had experiences we wish we could forget.

Our counseling services were peer-based and feminist. We were trained in hotline protocols, but there were no certifications and no trigger warnings. We were survivors swapping stories, talking about how we were coping, and building theory from our practices. I learned an entire vocabulary for what happened to victims: childhood sexual abuse, incest, stalking, street harassment, battering, rape culture. The most healing conversations were always spontaneous. Someone might be triggered by a hotline call, and their rush of emotional outpouring would infuse us all, leading even the most reticent to share details of their assaults. We stoked each other's outrage while offering what meager comfort we could.

The Center was one of several anti-rape organizations to pioneer the concept of a "safe space" by creating a setting for victims to recount their experiences in which they would never be questioned or disbelieved. We were determined to challenge the institutionalized skepticism for victims' stories displayed by the police, medical personnel, politicians, the media, and society. We were establishing a basic premise: that women deserved not to be raped, full stop. It was a radically transformative concept at a time when victim-blaming was the norm. After encountering endless questions about what rape victims wore, drank, or said, we were determined to center the blame on the men who committed the assaults. Women deserved lives free of sexual violence, we believed, not because women were men's mothers, daughters, wives, and sisters, but because they were individuals with the same universal human rights to bodily safety and freedom that men expected to enjoy.

Now, in retrospect, I realize that this victim-centering also led to overpromising. We did not yet understand that while each survivor has a truth based on their experiences, this trauma-informed perspective may be one of several coexisting truths, all based on different interpretations of the facts of the event. Over the decades, as victim-centering spread into the broader culture, it became heresy to many to ask for due process or to ever question survivor accounts. We had overcorrected. In our call out culture today, the concept of a safe space has been distorted to prohibit anything that might evoke feelings of discomfort, as if all pain—by definition—is a violation.

Many of these conversations with other volunteers were painfully uncomfortable because I could never anticipate how a word, a smell, or a vision would retrigger my trauma. And yet the more I shared my stories, the less they frightened me. As I healed, I became less afraid of my emotions.

It was in these sessions that I found the words to attach to my experiences. I was finally able to talk about my rapes beyond what I'd hesitantly revealed to my boyfriend. Many people don't realize that an extended childhood is a privilege denied to many childhood sexual abuse survivors. I shared how it felt to be violently jerked out of innocence. The abrupt transition from child to survivor that happens in seconds takes a lifetime to process.

Only through telling my stories could I finally understand that I was not at fault in the encounters that had rerouted my life. Only through sharing could I understand that my conservative, religious family had hoped that keeping me ignorant would mean keeping me safe, although my mother surely knew better. Decades later, she would confide in me that she too had been a victim of incest—in the 1930s, from age eight to sixteen—by her uncle who lived in the large farmhouse shared by our extended family. She'd turned down a local college scholarship to escape into marriage, which had also completely reconfigured her life. She hadn't known how to share this information with me when I was going through my incoherent feelings of shame and self-blame.

I had to work hard to make sure that my rage didn't damage me or those around me, particularly my son, Howard. By the time I took over as executive director of the Rape Crisis Center in 1979 after Nkenge Touré stepped down, he was old enough to ask tough questions. How could I explain to my beloved child that his father is a pedophile I hope he never meets? I wrestled with my conscience every day as he grew taller and began to resemble his father. I knew he deserved unconditional love from his mother; being born was not his fault nor was my decision to keep him. But by the time I received Fuller's letter, I was exhausted from trying to keep my rage at my absent rapist in check.

Fuller's letter sparked a furious debate about whether we were going to respond to his request for help. We were a staff of predominantly Black women. We weren't surprised that rapes occurred in prisons because we already knew that sexual assaults were more about domination and power than sexual pleasure. But what could an organization dedicated to helping rape victims do for a rapist?

After months of indecision, I finally decided to go to the prison because Fuller offered me hope. But it wasn't just that. I wanted to find answers to why I was hurting so bad. Hurt people *do* hurt people, and I was no different. Even my approach to Fuller was jumbled with anger, pain, and yearning. I wanted to make him deal with my pain; part of me wanted to lay into him, to punish him, because my rapists had never been punished. But I also wanted to see if I could change him, to make it impossible for him to hurt anyone else again. He mentioned in his letter that he was still raping men. Could he be convinced to stop?

No one else from the Center wanted to go, so I was alone in seeking answers to questions I didn't fully know I had. I went to witness his abject remorse. I wanted to compel him to admit that however horrible things were in prison, his situation was all his fault. I wanted to feel power—the brave survivor confronting the murderous rapist who deserved everything he got. In my false bravado, I didn't foresee the possibility that this encounter would challenge and change me as well.

When I went through that final locked door in Lorton and entered the prison meeting room, six men awaited me. I'd been expecting one man, Fuller, and even he I didn't know how to picture. I was taken aback. It wasn't just how many there were; it was how big they were. I didn't anticipate that they would be so physically intimidating, like buffed-up MMA fighters. Only years later did I realize that I was meeting the prison's predators: the men who bulked their bodies up to avoid becoming prey.

They were sitting in a circle, calmly dressed in civilian clothes instead of prison jumpsuits. I didn't know what to say beyond "Hi." I felt supremely out of place. But one man spoke up and took the lead. He was William Fuller, he said, and he introduced the man sitting next to him as Larry Cannon. The pair had started the group that was now sitting before me, which they called Prisoners Against Rape.

Fuller didn't seem alarmed at my wide-eyed confusion. He just kept talking, introducing me to the group and its mission. He spoke about "rape culture" and how they wanted to change how they viewed women. I'd heard the term "rape culture" before, but never from the mouths of Black men and never from men convicted of sexual assault. I began to realize that they had been changing themselves long before they reached out to the Center. I exhaled for what felt like the first time since I'd entered the prison.

At first, they only shared their experiences in broad terms like "I mistreated women" or "I was convicted of raping women." I didn't question their vagueness. After all, people rarely perceive themselves as villains in their own stories, and abusers frequently minimize what they've done. Besides, I didn't want the graphic details.

After those who wanted to speak had introduced themselves, Fuller asked if I was willing to help them learn about things like feminism, Black history, and violence against women. I think I'd already decided to work with them. However, I felt it was important to spell out my nonnegotiable rules. I told them that I would not be writing letters to parole boards on their behalf. I would not be the slightest bit patient with any romantic overtures. And I would not be bringing in anything from outside—no drugs or clothes or cigarettes. Only books.

They all nodded in agreement. I couldn't detect any disappointment in their faces, but perhaps they were good at hiding their reactions. And so, I began teaching Black feminist theory to rapists, my first calling in project. I instinctively approached their wrongdoing with accountability and education, hoping that they could change if given a chance. I didn't have a name for it then; I just knew I had to try to make a difference.

In the early sessions, I tried to hide my fear. I didn't precisely feel unsafe, because there were alert prison guards just outside the door. But I did not want to appear hypervigilant as a result of my PTSD, constantly expecting to be raped again. I took comfort in knowing these men were never getting out; they were serving life sentences. I tried to remember that I could come and go, while they could not. But I also didn't feel relaxed.

At the Center, we often began with our truths. So, in that first session, after setting my guidelines, I fell back on the only real thing I could be sure of: my own story. That's what we did at the Crisis Center: telling our stories, hoping to be believed, hoping we could change how women were treated. I shared the story of the incest that led to my pregnancy; how angry I was about what happened to me; how I'd had to overcome my anger and fear to meet with them. I quipped that working at the Center meant that we risked getting a skewed perception of men. Even though I was fortunate to have five brothers and a great father, and I knew all men weren't monsters, I'd still heard so many horror stories over the hotline. Yet there I was.

I'm not sure whether my story opened the floodgates, the way hotline calls had for us volunteers. Or maybe they wanted to assure me of my safety. But, slowly, several of the men started resharing their own stories, going deeper. One said he'd been raped as a child and wanted to hurt people like he'd been hurt. One admitted he'd not only raped a woman but also sodomized her with a broom handle, killing her. That's the story that shook me to my core; I still shake today from that dreadful image.

Finally, one of the men said he raped other men who were incarcerated with him. After that confession, the room went silent. As I looked around the room, I suspected all of them had done the same, or been victims themselves. Lorton warehoused teen boys as well as adult men, and the stronger preyed on the weaker. Since all of them had entered Lorton as teenagers, they continued the cycle until they chose not to.

That's when I felt their desperation. I didn't question why hearing the sordid details of the violence they'd inflicted somehow made me feel safer. Go figure. I can only surmise they admitted their crimes to build trust. No one was forcing them to be there. They came because they wanted to change, and I felt that. They ached to reclaim their humanity. Incarcerated people are rarely listened to. Society does not want to hear what happened to them, only what they've done to others. Prisoners Against Rape was their way of lifting their voices as victimized violators, to bring attention to their pain as well as their crimes.

So began my weekly journeys to Lorton, a tradition that lasted three transformative years. I looked forward to Fridays as the capstone of my week. Working with the prisoners in what became an informal book club provided an intellectually stimulating break from the stress of maintaining a barely viable nonprofit organization. I felt I spent too much time seeking grants and donations, managing staff and budgets, negotiating with police and hospitals about how victims were treated, and representing the organization to politicians, donors, and the media. As the executive director, I was removed from the more fulfilling day-to-day counseling services. Going to Lorton began to recharge my enthusiasm for the work and reinforced my optimism that we could make a difference—that we could prevent sexual assaults.

Sometimes others from the Center joined me on visits, like Nkenge Touré or Yulanda Ward. They admitted that they didn't go on that first trip because they wanted to see if I came out safe. When I told them what happened, they shared my fascination with this informal experiment: Could we convince men not to rape? We had no special training or insight, but we and the prisoners bonded as fellow survivors. We witnessed their pain as well as their joy. They had grown from boys to men in prison, and now they were adults experiencing regrets and seeking better futures. Many of those Fridays were filled with as much laughter as learning.

They learned to listen to women's voices; I learned to widen my perception of men who rape. These men I saw each Friday seemed like a brotherhood, supporting one another emotionally and perhaps physically as well. If one person had a pack of cigarettes, they shared instead of hoarding them. While I could never fathom all they'd experienced, I could see their excitement at learning new things together as we lifted each other's consciousness and explored Black feminist theory. I didn't know who we were until we discovered what we could do together. The work built the relationships instead of the relationships building the work. We stumbled, sometimes harming each other, but we learned to move beyond our comfort zones together.

Soon, I was invited to join them on Family Visitor Day. It was like a Fourth of July celebration without fireworks, hosted on the large grass-covered quad in the center of the minimum-security area. The tables were covered with white tablecloths and filled with food. Wives, girlfriends, children, and other family and friends arrived in their most festive summer outfits to share brief moments with their loved ones behind bars. It was a chance for them to feel like they could live normal lives, with laughter and tears affirming relationships that endured under the most constricted of circumstances.

When strange things happened during these family visits, the men quickly encircled me to protect me from noticing something a little off; I was warned never to look under a tablecloth that was rapidly moving with no wind. The skirted tables were their "bedrooms." I only later realized the irony of a rape survivor being surrounded by six rapists and feeling protected. They treated me as a smart little sister whom they had to respect and guard at the same time.

I'm not certain when the emotional shift in my relationship with the men occurred. But as I delighted in the joy of shared learning and mutual growth, I forgot to be angry and afraid. I learned that my anger at them was largely born of fear, and eliminating the fear dissipated the anger. Perhaps I was able to relate to the men in Lorton because, when I first passed through those gates, I'd felt caged within myself. Maybe it was because I'd been caged at that home for unwed mothers.

Whatever the cause, I discovered a capacity for trust under the most improbable of circumstances. I learned to see the humanity of those I had only previously seen as predators. They had seemed nothing but evil to me until they helped me see them in all their complexities, with all their challenges and contradictions. By the end of our sessions, I appreciated and respected them as co-conspirators working to end rape.

I now realize that working with Prisoners Against Rape was my first experience with the power of calling in. My instinct, when William Fuller wrote, was one of rage and disgust. If I'd fired back an outraged letter, I would've just slammed the door and spread more pain. It was only my desperation that led me to risk visiting Lorton.

But doing so became a lucky breakthrough. I began to question my judgmentalism and quick dismissal of others. I learned that my fears could be managed, that they weren't always my fiercest protectors, and that they did not have to stop me from doing what I believed was right. This lesson wouldn't transform me right away; I'd still need to make plenty of mistakes to become who I am today. But this experience was now invisibly tattooed in my heart, leading me toward the philosophy of calling in.

So, what do I mean by the phrase "Calling In"?

We are all constantly making choices about how we walk through life, choosing how we interact with the people we meet—whether it's in person or online, whether we agree with them or disagree. The choices people make are often limited by the choices they believe they have. But instead of telling you how to live your life, I'd rather tell you how I'm trying to live mine.

For much of my life, I had no real trust or patience for others. I reacted with fear or domination, caring only about protecting myself. I would call out others at the drop of a hat—whether it was for a real insult or an honest mistake. I was a loaded shotgun, looking for an excuse to pull the trigger. And I had to *learn* to be different—to approach others with less anger and a little more love.

That's the simple definition: a call in is a call out done with love.

After months of talking with the Center's counselor, trying to explain how my trauma was scorching me inside, I knew I wanted to practice "compassionate politics" and improve my emotional literacy to better align my feelings with my integrity. At the most despairing moment in my life, I was learning that I had choices—and I wanted to learn how to choose better ones, ones that represented who I was inside. I'd been letting my fears compromise my integrity. I didn't like that; I wanted to do something different.

We all have a choice. If a coworker says something inappropriate, we can respond with scorn. Or we can approach them with patience and empathy, asking about the feelings or thoughts that led them to use hurtful language or to be so judgmental. In both situations, the harm is not ignored, because we don't want the harm to continue. We need our colleagues to know they shouldn't say that again. But in choosing to call in, our response is contoured by love instead of anger. Asking the coworker to tell you more begins to develop your relationship.

It's a simple switch, but it can pick the lock of distrust and defensiveness, which springs open whole rooms and corridors. Even if the only concrete outcome is to set up the next conversation, this is a win. Conversation enables an empathetic connection to build and with it the potential for solidarity and growth. And our confidence in navigating this sort of conflict will improve with practice.

"The practice of compassionate neutrality in a world of reactions is powerful," attests communications expert Tatiana Apandi Anacki. People respond more strongly to a negative emotion than a positive one, which is why we obsess over criticism and deflect praise. Compassionate neutrality offers balance, withholding judgment while providing positive encouragement. This is what happened in my conversations with William Fuller and the men of Prisoners Against Rape.

Those Friday lessons taught me the power of listening to difficult, triggering stories without judgment and with curiosity. Listening became a practice vital not only to understanding others but also to understanding myself. I'd thought I was protecting myself by walling myself off from emotionally challenging situations, but I was actually weakening myself. By choosing instead to listen and share, I found unexpected connections and unexpected relief.

In the process, I learned not to be afraid of my secrets. My shame and regrets held me back from owning all of my experiences as the joy of growth. Sharing these secrets began my process of healing. My pain gave away my power. But just because I'd forgotten my power didn't mean it was gone.

Calling in, for me, began as a skill that I needed to practice. It was work I was doing on and for myself. Do I want to act today out of anger or shame, or with love and grace? Do I want to be imprisoned by what has happened to me or to self-determine how I will be in the world? That choice was rarely easy to make, but I started from a place of *never* being able to make it.

We can learn to transmute the hurts and fears inside us. We may always have these emotions, but we don't always have to be controlled by them. Our first instinct may be to lob pain back to someone who has hurt us—but why should we let the actions of someone else disturb our emotional balance so much? I've learned that my first thought reveals my instincts. My second thought reveals my values. Gaining control over my life and my responses is important to becoming and presenting the person I want to be proud of.

Through calling in, I can be stubborn in a way that lives up to my higher values. I can refuse to express my pain by passing it on to someone else. I can refuse to grant someone my burden of anger unless I *know* they deserve it. As the Greek philosopher Aristotle said, "Anybody can become angry—that is easy, but to be angry with the right person and to the right degree and at the right time and for the right purpose, and in the right way—that is not within everybody's power and is not easy." I want to be precise with my anger.

Calling in depends on the rigorous practice of self-reflection and critical thinking. I wanted to learn how to practice empathetic accountability. Developing emotional and intellectual fitness requires entertaining contradictory thoughts at the same time, so that I can question my assumptions and generously consider other viewpoints— although remember that consideration is not necessarily agreement.

Another way to understand calling in is as "accountability culture" or "survivors' justice." It's not about feeling sorry for wrongdoers but about recognizing their humanity, in the same way we protect the humanity of victims. It's about engaging in constructive—not destructive—conflict with each other. It's about learning together to be less judgmental, more generous, more collaborative, and more appreciative of nuance and ambiguity. Do we want to silence those who make us think differently about things? Or do we want to engage in conversations that can hold multiple truths at the same time? We can hold people accountable using love, forgiveness, and respect, giving people room to grow—because they may be capable of changing. We can say what we mean and mean what we say, but we don't have to say it mean. That's a choice.

I began to understand these ideas well before I had a word for them. I only learned the phrase "Calling In" decades later. It was coined in 2013 by Ngọc Loan Trần, a then eighteen-year-old Việt/mixed-race trans writer and activist. Loan was writing from a different time and place, frustrated by the impatience and casual cruelty they saw online and in person, as progressive activists fought among themselves. As they explained:

> I picture "Calling In" as a practice of pulling folks back in who have strayed from us . . . a practice of loving each other enough to allow each other to make mistakes, a practice of loving ourselves enough to know that what we're trying to do here is a radical unlearning of everything we have been configured to believe is normal.

Loan's essay transformed how I saw many of the techniques I had stumbled upon over the decades. These weren't just tools for healing my relationship with hate, insecurity, and anger. They were tools that everyday folks needed to be able to put into practice. Loan was asking all of us to build the human rights culture that's so desperately needed: one where *how* we do the work is as important as the work we do because *who* we bring along is inseparable from how far we'll go.

Calling in begins with healing our relationships with ourselves and others, which requires radical forgiveness and radical love. And it grows from there. Calling in asks us to call on our better and braver selves, even in the most painful and hateful situations. It's a chance to decide how you're going to live your life, as part of deciding what is a life worth living. I've found embodying calling in to be a lifelong learning process.

Activism is the art of making your life matter. It's about discovering that you can achieve contentment and happiness by serving others. But changing people's hearts and minds can take a long time, so sustainable activism requires a change in perspective. Embracing the principles of calling in can help you avoid becoming a burned-out movement tourist.

As I looked back, I realized that all of the successful organizations and movements I'd been a part of had been able to succeed because they adopted the tenets of calling in before we'd even been able to put a name to these practices. Calling in builds bridges and connections so we can grow together. It leads to alliances that make inclusion and collaboration the norm, bringing people together without letting differences grind us down.

Calling in is a philosophy of social change that's both old and new, one that I believe is uniquely suited to this moment in the twenty-first century in a similar way to how nonviolence defined the civil rights movement of the twentieth century. Dr. Martin Luther King Jr. spoke in 1968 of a "militant nonviolence" that could "bring the coalition of conscience together." I believe that many on the Left still fail to understand how powerful nonviolent tactics can be. We need to stop inflicting verbal and emotional violence on one another. The Reverend Doctor Joseph Lowery, another wise icon who was called the dean of the civil rights movement, was famous for saying, "Let's turn *to* each other, not *on* each other."

The needs of the country and the planet are crying out for us. But we can't help with a worn-out brigade that's constantly sniping at one another. We need to strengthen our skills for talking beyond our bubbles. We need to rebuild trust in our communities and our institutions. We want to be trusted . . . but does our behavior inspire trust?

Calling in is not a better way to tell someone they are wrong. Its purpose is to create the conditions for differences of opinion to be heard, to allow facts to be ascertained, and to avoid ideological rigidity and political bullying. Its purpose is to prepare us to have difficult conversations—with our families, our classmates, our colleagues, our neighbors, and our friends. It can prepare us to take things a little slower, assume folks are not trying to be assholes, and try what Jamaicans call "reasoning" with each other. We can talk instead of fussing over differences that may not be that big a deal in the face of the larger crises facing our society. We can refuse to derail conversations simply because we're uncomfortable or challenged to grow. We will either learn how to work better together, or our society will disintegrate into warring factions that will destroy this democratic experiment called America.

I learned some of this from traveling to thirty-odd countries, enough that I needed a new passport even after the State Department had already added extra pages to the first one to extend its life. In my travels, I've discovered that most people are remarkably similar: they just want to take care of themselves and their families, do the right things, and get along in life. They're friendly when you're friendly. Sure, there are mean people everywhere, but they are always the minority. We need to learn how to talk to each other without our guards up, looking for a reason to pounce. When I meet people with short fuses looking for a chance to be offended, I wonder why they keep making choices that don't seem to bring them any joy. If those grudges you're carrying aren't making you happier, why don't you consider letting them go?

Most people want a sense of belonging. They want to feel like they're a part of something important and empowering, something that gives their life and their suffering meaning. They want to feel valued and to believe that they're adding value to society. Let's welcome them into our movements for justice.

As expert movement builders Kelly Hayes and Mariame Kaba remind us, "Movement building requires a culture of listening." None of us has all the knowledge necessary to defeat the oppressive system under which we live, this status quo that's harmful to everyone. So let's look beyond our individual experiences and identities. We increase the risk of violence if we become convinced that those who don't align with us pose an existential threat to everything we hold dear.

It is not foolish to believe that things will get better. As Audre Lorde recognizes, social change is "like the volcano . . . in any revolutionary process there is a period of intensification and a period of explosion." We're living through a period of intensification right now, a period of anger and distrust and fear. Calling in will help us harness our energies to make the explosion powerful enough to change the world for the better.

Of course, to reach our grand goals, we need to start with many smaller steps. We need to start by asking ourselves some practical questions: W\hat do you say to call someone in? When is calling someone in the right thing to do and when is calling out warranted? How intent should we be on changing others? How can we heal ourselves so that we're ready to call others in? Which cultural blowups should you wade into and which should you ignore? Can we really come together and create a cultural shift? And can we hope to stay focused on the goals that matter?

The chapters to come will address these questions and more. But first, a more immediate one: What about William Fuller? Did he change?

Ten years after I'd left the Rape Crisis Center, I was walking down a street in DC when I heard a bass voice shouting my name. I turned, and there he was: William Fuller rushing toward me, out from behind bars. For years, this had been my nightmare; I'd only been able to sleep when I first got home from Lorton because I knew that none of the men would ever be released. Even after we'd grown friendly, I still felt a jolt of terror at seeing Fuller on the street.

I could tell he wanted to hug me, but he held back. I was grateful that he'd listened to me enough in years past to know that a woman's space is her own.

In a gush of words, he told me everything: he had been paroled, he had gotten married, and he was working in construction now. He lifted his little lunch box as if to prove it. He looked good, I realized, grounded. He told me that he was continuing to read and had gone back to school. He thanked me for all the work we'd done together; he told me I'd changed his life.

As he walked on, I was left shaken and with a strange thought. I hadn't changed *him*; he'd changed *me*. Or maybe neither thought was right. He'd already been on his path, and I'd just helped him along. I'd already had the potential to overcome my fears, but I needed someone else to show me how. We each needed someone else to call us in as we struggled to figure out where we could go and who we could be. If we just had a little more space, a little more grace.

2.

THE USES AND ABUSES OF CALL OUTS

Movement building isn't about finding your tribe—it's about growing your tribe across difference to focus on a common set of goals.

—Alicia Garza

One day in the winter of 1974, I came home to my apartment building in the Adams Morgan neighborhood of DC and found a notice posted on the door. All tenants had ninety days to vacate, it read. Just a shade more polite than "GET OUT." Our building was being converted into condominiums. Below the notice, someone had taped a handwritten note: "Let's meet in the laundry room tonight. This isn't right."

When I walked into the laundry room later that evening, I found the room full of other tenants, mostly venting. I offered to take notes at the meeting because someone had to. And before I knew it, I was tenant president. I was just a twenty-one-year-old single mother in a studio apartment. A Howard University dropout who couldn't afford my senior year. A woman who worked nine to five as a secretary and five to nine as a cocktail waitress. But also, now, I was trying to save my whole apartment building from eviction.

Before long, I connected with a tenant organizing group called the City Wide Housing Coalition that helped unsavvy tenants like me figure out how to fight back against predatory landlords. Soon, I was attending City Wide meetings regularly, which led to a set of Sunday gatherings for a reading group called the DC Study Group, where a dozen of us studied leftist thinkers and translated their teachings into activism. City Wide was one of the study group's offshoots, as was the Southern Africa Support Project, which became the Free South Africa movement, one of the biggest anti-apartheid mobilizations in the United States. I stumbled through the door, but I ended up sticking with the study group for years. Meeting Nkenge Touré at City Wide would lead me to the Rape Crisis Center, which sparked my formal emergence as a political activist.

That was the political magic of DC's "Chocolate City" in the mid-1970s. It was a period of bubbling opportunity and unlikely connections, where new progressive ideas felt not just possible but realistic. And then—unable to resist the allure of shouting each other down—I saw the Left's power in DC dissipate before our eyes.

Our optimism was based on having at last achieved Home Rule, which let us use our own tax dollars on priorities we felt were important. Until 1973, the nation's capital had been governed by a subcommittee of Congress, but the Home Rule Act granted control to residents, who could at last elect their own mayor and city council. In a city that was 70 percent Black and liberal, this felt like a door swinging open. Anyone who wanted to become involved could now consider policies that would've gone nowhere just a couple of years earlier.

During this heady period, more senior citizen housing went up in just a few years than in the past four decades, and every child in the DC public school system was guaranteed a summer job. My son became a projectionist at movie theaters, which taught him skills he'd benefit from his whole life. He later became a structural and mechanical engineer. The summer-jobs program reduced crime, improved student literacy, and increased vital city services by renovating community parks, swimming pools, tennis courts, and recreation centers. We were beginning to enjoy amenities that people in the suburbs took for granted.

Across the city, new progressive groups were forming, and older leftist organizations were reconvening. A new political party, the DC Statehood Party, had emerged in 1971 as an option to the left of the Democratic Party. The Statehood Party advocated for long-overdue voting rights and educational reforms. Then there were contingents of firmly leftist groups—like the Socialist Workers Party, the Communist Workers Party, and the Revolutionary Communist Party. I didn't join any of these more radical formations, but their presence was felt in our community organizing.

I remember sitting in a living room each Sunday, listening not to the gospel but to the study group's leader, Jimmy Garrett, as we discussed the potential improvements that were now within the grasp of working-class Black residents of DC: fair housing, funded schools, real voting rights, representation in Congress. Our activist coalitions wouldn't just transform the city, we could shift national politics. Winning congressional representatives for a city whose license plates still bear the grim joke "End Taxation Without Representation" would mean two more progressives in Congress.

Those study group meetups certainly *felt* like gospel: it was obvious to us that the 1970s could be a transformative decade for Chocolate City. But instead, I watched that window of possibility quickly shut, with little to show for it. Instead of collaborating, that loose coalition of mostly white leftist groups turned on each other, developing a culture of narrow critique and vicious call outs, which blunted progress on issue after issue.

The building for which I became tenant president did succeed in shutting down the landlord's hasty eviction, and residents eventually rallied to buy the building outright. But larger victories on housing and other priorities were elusive. I remember standing in a public meeting, advocating for protections for tenants across the city—expanding DC's first citywide rent control bill—only to watch the hall devolve into a swarm of bickering over procedure and power. In that moment of turmoil, it was as if residents' lives were less important than who got to bang the gavel.

Instead of developing a functioning alliance, many of the leftist groups became what community organizer Betita Martinez has termed "everybody's-wrong-except-us" organizations. I saw how extreme confidence and aggressiveness by people convinced of their self-righteousness could disrupt an entire movement, especially if they didn't realize or care about the consequences of their actions. Even as a young and headstrong activist, I was repelled by organizations that spent more time warring with one another than resolving practical problems. And that's what I witnessed.

The Socialist Workers Party and the Communist Workers Party would regularly debate about the arcane differences that separated them: whether Cuba, the Soviet Union, or China had the better application of communist principles; whether Lenin or Marx or Trotsky was more important. They would write vicious (and often boring) screeds, each group denouncing the other as the *real* "fascist, racist, bourgeois pigs." They debated about dead white men instead of thinking of the poor Black residents around them. All the while, their opponents were content to label each group "communist" and move on.

Sometimes our stubbornness about being right fulfills a psychological need and lowers our anxiety. We like poking holes in others' thinking, resulting in a competition of who can criticize more. This semantic violence can be preferred over actual changes in the distribution of power, resulting in symbolic statements rather than real changes in power relationships.

None of this internecine fighting won over a single opponent; nor did it bring on board a new wave of working-class Washingtonians. Instead, the backbiting, call out–ridden culture kept outsiders *outside*. Feminist writer Jo Freeman wrote an article in *Ms.* magazine in 1976 describing this behavior as "character assassination which amounts to psychological rape . . . done to disparage and destroy." Who'd want to join an organization that'd treat you like that?

It's no surprise, then, that issues like fair housing, voting rights, and statehood all languished. Plenty of people in the capital and around the country sympathized with even the loftiest of these issues—the prospect of DC becoming a state, or at least gaining representatives in Congress. Even President Jimmy Carter openly advocated for granting DC congressional representatives. But, apparently, this wasn't enough. Different progressive factions kept fighting to get *their* version of a plan endorsed, to the point where the DC Statehood Party actively campaigned *against* a constitutional amendment that would give DC its own congresspeople. Why? Because it fell short of full statehood.

As each faction postured and squabbled, the energy of the era evaporated. The right-wing opposition firmed up its position, and in 1980 Ronald Reagan swept into power, with a congressional majority to back him up. Reagan's Congress had zero interest in expanding DC's independence. Instead, it aggressively stepped in to veto *local* DC laws, including a 1981 sexual assault law that aimed to decriminalize sodomy and homosexuality within the city and make it legal for wives to file rape charges against their husbands. This small step was too much for the badly named Moral Majority. And, by law, Congress still had the power to veto DC laws, so it did—pushing the district back to the functional status of a colony.

With that, the bright window for progress that we'd imagined in the mid-1970s had slammed shut. Liberals and progressives had taken their massive majority in the city and squandered it. We spent all our time fighting rather than building a movement to cement the gains that were possible.

We didn't understand back then that coalitions are, by definition, composed of people who have different ideas, tactics, and strategies but who work together to achieve a common goal. We didn't realize that being united was more important than being right. Our infighting took our eyes off our opponents. Instead of retreating, they regrouped.

The lesson I eventually learned was that call outs might have their place and purpose, but they can also be distracting, even destructive. I didn't recognize this until I saw the Reagan era bring all our progress to a halt. Only hindsight is 20/20, of course. But this history has made me pay closer attention to the trends I've been seeing among progressives in the last decade. I've seen American politics start to resemble that little cell of leftist DC groups. We've come to embrace calling out as a tool for accomplishing change—and it can be. Calling out is such an easy muscle to flex. But as I've learned, it's a limited tool, one that's a poor fit for a lot of jobs. Calling out can be an interesting way to expend a whole lot of anguish to achieve very little.

Still, I believe it's important for activists to understand all the tools at our disposal, how to wield them, and when to wield them. So, what *is* a call out for? When is it the right tool, and when is it wrong? Because there *are* appropriate uses of call outs.

The Purpose of a Call Out

Public call outs have long been employed by activists and dissidents, well before the phrase "call out" was ever coined. Our concentrated fury is one of the few means held by the powerless to bring the powerful to account, which helps explain why so many activists today perceive it as the most powerful tool they have—especially as a way of drawing dramatic attention to urgent priorities. We wield the handful of tools that money can't buy or break: our voice, our experience, our courage, our resolve, our anger. To quote writer Zora Neale Hurston, we "speak so that you can speak again."

What else are so many of the revolutionary moments in human rights history except call outs? When Martin Luther could no longer stomach the excesses of the Renaissance Catholic Church, he posted his ninety-five theses to a door of the Castle Church in Wittenberg. When the American colonists had lost faith in the English monarchy, they challenged King George with the Declaration of Independence. When Frederick Douglass escaped slavery, he made it his mission to publicly highlight the cruelty and hypocrisy of the peculiar institution for all Americans to see by publishing an abolitionist newspaper and giving speeches around the country. When Elizabeth Cady Stanton reached her last nerve as a subservient housewife in 1848, she wrote the Seneca Falls Declaration to call out the abuses suffered by nineteenth-century women at the hands of men.

Each of these documents was incendiary, timeless—and lucky to be taken up, reprinted, and disseminated far and wide. But as time has passed, media has gotten faster. The last two decades have super-charged the potential for change, as internet outrage has organized movements of millions at unprecedented speed. The many accusers who found common voices in the #MeToo movement can attest to the power of the call out culture in bringing down powerful figures entrenched in well-protected industries and institutions. So have the many participants in the Black Lives Matter movement, which brought together more than 23 million marchers to demonstrate their outrage at the impunity with which police and vigilantes kill unarmed Black men and women.

These examples are just a few of the many social movements that have sprung from the power of the internet and social media. Never before have average individuals held the raw power to reach *so* many people, simply by writing or filming their thoughts and sending them out to the world. For that matter, never before have vulnerable people been allowed to be publicly angry without severe punishment. The democratically distributed nature of such call outs has itself been revolutionary. As author Ta-Nehisi Coates wrote, "Until recently, cancellation flowed exclusively downward, from the powerful to the powerless. But now, in this era of fallen gatekeepers, where anyone with a Twitter handle or Facebook account can be a publisher, banishment has been ostensibly democratized."

But to understand where the tool of the call out can be most con-structive, it's important to look at what these successful call outs have in common.

Call outs are most effective when they target powerful people beyond our reach and when public scrutiny is a strategic weapon we deploy against the unreachably powerful. Criticizing such people is an important tactic for democratizing justice when appeals to democratic institutions appear futile. The viral amplification of social media can help people facing structural inequalities overcome their sense of powerlessness, making it feel as if long-held hierarchies of power are finally being subverted.

People with privilege often minimize the necessity of call out culture as a tool for achieving accountability. They'll criticize human rights activists as "unforgiving, spiteful keyboard warriors"—but calling out, when justified, is done not out of spite but out of an awareness of the elusiveness of justice. While sometimes these call outs are only symbolic gestures, they're better than nothing. After all, they're the only consequence we control.

Calling out, then, is often an appropriate tactic for checking those in power who are betraying the public trust, particularly elected officials or de facto leaders. When ex-president Donald Trump enacted policies to divide America, cover up his own corruption, and flout constitutional limits on presidential power, he deserved to be called out, loudly and publicly, by his fellow citizens. Likewise, corporate officials who quietly destroy the environment while exploiting people's labor deserve to be called out because public shaming may be the best strategy for holding them accountable. You can only really boycott a product if you were previously in the habit of purchasing that product—whereas public shaming broadens the number of people who can get involved.

Other justified uses of shame campaigns include warnings about predators, rapists, and abusers who seek to get away with violating others. In this instance, exposure is a way to protect the community in desperate situations where abusers are shielded and victims' voices are devalued. In the 1970s, anti-rape activists used "zap" actions like distributing posters of rapists because we believed that most people who report rapes are telling the truth; only a tiny minority are acting maliciously. Call outs in such situations are riskier; they depend on accurate information to succeed. But they're often justified when other means of recourse have fallen on deaf ears.

The potential for inaccuracy is a valid criticism of overly hasty call outs. But one of the most common criticisms of call outs—that they're loud and disruptive—is a red herring. Courtesy isn't a luxury valued by those who most need the power and protection of call outs. We rightfully resist demands that we be polite to our oppressors when voicing our outrage and apologize in the "right" tone. F that! We won't calmly forgive them for wounds that won't heal because the injuries have not stopped. There may be other grounds to object to call outs—but politeness ain't it.

So, when *is* calling out a critical tool?

I'd argue that the following circumstances can justify a call out:

- When serious harm or wrongs have been committed.
- When confronting a major power disparity.
- When other means of recourse have failed or are inaccessible.
- When doing so will prevent others from experiencing similar future harms.
- When doing so will help others who've suffered similar past harms come forward.
- When the individual or institution has a pattern of failing to address its wrongs.
- When trust and good faith have already been exhausted.

My point is that there are many times when call outs should be used. In these carefully calibrated instances, call outs are the best tool we have. But as seasoned human rights activists can attest, the call out is not the tool of first resort; it's the last resort after other tactics have failed—a "in case of emergency, break glass" tactic.

Can Call Outs Be Justified?

Of course, not everyone believes that call outs or "cancellation" can ever be justified.

A majority of Americans agree that "cancel culture" is a problem that should be addressed. But we can't agree on what "being canceled" means or who should wield the hook to yank someone offstage. Since people get criticized and fired all the time, it's difficult to distinguish between routine behavior and situations that deserve our condemnation. And so the debate over free speech and harmful speech precipitates echo chambers instead of solutions.

It doesn't help that we're living in an "age of offense-taking," as political philosopher Mikael Good and policy expert Philip Wallach wrote. Being offended to justify being offensive carries political cachet; Trump rode the emotional catharsis of outrage all the way to the White House. And aggressive victimhood is a familiar ploy by right-wingers who push at the limits of free speech and then claim victimhood when the people they punch down on fight back.

Despite their uproar over cancel culture, extremist conservatives have been the chief drivers of cancel culture in the United States. Just look at which lawmakers have enacted laws to push transgender Americans and immigrants out of public life by making it more difficult for people to transition and barring immigrants from many Muslim-majority countries. Look at who's been wielding threats to arrest or assassinate ordinary people just doing their jobs—librarians, judges, poll workers, investigators, school administrators—and blowing up peoples' lives with attacks on their characters, livelihoods, and, sometimes, their children. I think the Right's furor over cancel culture is bullshit; it's hypocritical, selective, and opportunistic. The same conservatives who made criticizing the "oppressive" cancel culture the focus of their 2020 presidential convention quickly pivoted to limiting what colleges and universities can teach.

In response to this "anti-woke" backlash from the Right and center, the Left has inherited the awkward position of trying to defend cancel culture as what journalist Ernest Owens called "an essential means of democratic expression and accountability." Most often, we insist that conservatives are panicked over nothing. Writer Roxane Gay argued in 2021 that cancel culture "is the bogeyman that people have come up with to explain away bad behavior." The Right wants a return to impunity, we say, while we merely want overdue justice.

But it's just not true that call outs only ever result in people getting what they deserve—especially when those call outs happen online. Because while call outs can happen in classrooms, in workplaces, or nearly anywhere human beings have conflicts with each other, there's a reason we tend to think of them as an online phenomenon. Social media amplifies human emotions, positive or negative, because its economic models are designed to capture our attention through outrage for profit. And while technology has made rapid leaps, our emotions have not. We're still prone to dominating, shaming, and punishing other people—just as in the days of public stocks, whipping posts, and duels. Social media has readily become a new outlet for all those impulses, amplified by easy anonymity, quickly written posts, and metrics that reward volume over accuracy. Difficult and brave things to say collide with easy and cowardly things to say; curiosity and patience are overrun by frustration and division. Critique becomes a public performance, one in which we react angrily to each other rather than debate critical issues. The point of protests becomes not to take a stand but to be seen taking a stand, while not taking a stand is perceived as an abandonment of political responsibility. It's as if we've taken that silence-equals-complicity formula to the extreme.

It's easier to build an outrage posse with a 280-character attention span than to construct a healing society of people who care about each other too much to choose to be cruel. And this online cruelty can produce offline outcomes because the internet is real and so are the people harmed by it. You don't need me to remind you that cyberbullying has led to suicides.

We've entered an era where freedom of speech is a privilege only for those who have sufficient social, cultural, or economic power to withstand attempts to cancel them. Life appears to go on for the "canceled" rich and powerful: corporations and celebrities. It's regular people—those who don't have expensive public relations firms to craft credible apologies—who have their lives upended. It may be the high school athlete who kneels during the national anthem. The museum curator who won't remove the Picassos. The uncle who won't stop watching *The Cosby Show* or listening to Michael Jackson. The neighbor who insists that women's sports should not be open to trans women. I know people who are reluctant to say they provide abortion services or live with people who have AIDS, or who teach in conservative states where speaking about certain topics could get them fired. People are even afraid to put out yard signs or display bumper stickers on their cars. Because no one goes back to a normal life after they've experienced a call out by an enraged mob. They will never have the same sense of safety after their lives have been exploded by trip wires they didn't expect.

In an atmosphere of easy outrage, it's not surprising that some on the Left employ this emotional weaponry, attracting negative attention from a subculture of well-meaning liberals and centrists for practicing the "politics of personal destruction." These purported allies blame call out culture primarily on identity politics, suggesting we're obsessed with isms and uncomfortable with intellectual diversity. But open inquiry and social justice values are not antithetical. Anyone who asserts that the primary problem in our democracy is illiberalism on the left—anyone who considers us "illiberal liberals"—seems not to have noticed that the bullets of political violence in our society nearly always travel from the right to the left.

To be clear, progressives are neither saints nor victims in the cancel wars. There are times we've insisted that artists be ignored, newspaper editors be dismissed, professors be fired, and students be expelled for daring to have opinions different from our accepted orthodoxy. There are times we've conflated being offended with being harmed and thrown around condemnatory buzzwords to justify our desire to punish opponents for *wrongthink*. There are times we've criticized people without considering mitigating circumstances. There are times we've refused to extend compassion to those we believe are undeserving. Lacking humility, there are times we've thought we'd reached a stage of advanced enlightenment that others would need to attain too before we could have substantive conversations with them.

The call out culture means you get to discriminate in favor of those who agree with you. But tribalism is still tribalism, whether Left or Right—and a call out culture makes our tribes smaller and more impotent. Loyalty to the tribe becomes more important than coexisting peacefully with others in a pluralistic system. And as millennial journalist Malikia Johnson pointed out, "being encapsulated within silos of their own thoughts" causes people "to mistakenly think that a larger part of the world agrees with their points of understanding." This part of cancel culture should be canceled.

What is missing in our distorted debate about cancel culture is that calling out is a powerful tool, but it *isn't* always the right tool for the job. Even when a call out is justified, it's not always productive. I've fired off my own call outs, only to watch them backfire, until I finally realized just how much hurt I was causing by my ignorance. And I've experienced the shame of being called out in turn. Shame weighs me down. I've had to learn not to be embarrassed when I make a mistake but to instead thank those who call me in and who appreciate my willingness to try again and do better. Because of the trauma I've experienced, feeling bad has a longer afterlife than feeling good. I can feel small or bad for a long time. But we don't have a long time.

Calling out can suck all the air out of a room and derail progress toward the goals that actually matter. Even in environments where 90 percent of us agree on 90 percent of issues, I've found that we're creating contagions of negativity in which rudeness is mistaken for rigor. We expect our allies to get everything right and to be perfectly aligned with our beliefs. But that's just not realistic.

A culture of calling out assumes that perfection is both knowable and achievable. Everyone who is not perfect is doing something wrong. But as Malikia Johnson observed, this perpetuates the same exclusive and hierarchical systems we're combatting; it becomes a privilege to be able to follow the conversation without being called out.

In this chapter, I want to explore the three main scenarios in which call outs just aren't effective and show why. But first, let's take a moment to be sure we understand how a call out starts and escalates. Because while we all know a call out when we see one, we don't really think too much about its defining characteristics.

The Anatomy of a Call Out

Most of us respond emotionally to call outs without thinking more deeply about their patterns and impacts. But as diversity expert Shakil Choudhury points out, we need to develop pattern recognition to successfully challenge call out culture, as understanding patterns is key to analyzing systems. Natalie Wynn, a trans podcasting star with a YouTube channel entitled ContraPoints, identifies the seven stages of a call out in a video explaining how call outs can become so quickly magnified. Here's a fictional, yet typical, story I tell to illustrate each stage.

Let's say you're gathering for a staff meeting at a social service organization. Joe, a white employee, has just made a cup of coffee and idly remarks that he's still getting used to the sounds of the inner city Black neighborhood he's moved into from the suburbs to be closer to work. "It's a bit jarring to hear so many police sirens, gunshots, and ambulances," he says. "It's keeping me up at night."

Also in the meeting is another employee, named Patricia. Patricia is Black and lives in this neighborhood. Her family has been there for generations, but they're being forced out by the same gentrification processes that brought Joe to the hood. In an amazingly short period of time, Patricia has watched grocery stores leave, hospitals shut down, fire departments relocate, and municipal services like fixing potholes or picking up trash disappear. Allegedly race-neutral economic decisions push people out of their communities, while cheaper housing, proximity to jobs, and public transportation pull in suburbanites like Joe. Once a neighborhood becomes white enough, municipal services magically reappear, along with the first Starbucks.

Patricia reacts heatedly to Joe's comments. The first stage of a call out occurs before she even opens her mouth, with a *presumption of guilt*, which contrasts with the presumption of innocence standard in courtrooms.

"Are you calling my neighborhood dangerous?" she says.

Immediately, the rest of the people in the room fall silent, not knowing how to react.

"No one invited you here," she continues. "And that's a racist thing to say!"

This next step is *abstraction*. The hurt revealed by Patricia's accusation is not necessarily based on an objective interpretation of what Joe said. But no one says "Whoa!" to slow the conversation down so that Joe is offered a chance to reconsider what he said based on the impact it had on Patricia. Nor is Patricia given an opportunity to explore what's underneath her explosion of pain. Instead, she's perceived as unreasonably angry and overly sensitive.

What next occurs is *essentialism*. The charge quickly metastasizes from Joe *said* something racist into Joe *is* a racist. This has become an attack on his moral character. Now Joe is also in pain, accused of biases he doesn't believe he has, with no chance to explain his intentions. Colleagues may quickly begin to change how they interact with Joe, as the limited information they can discern from this brief interaction—combined with their knowledge of Joe's and Patricia's identities—might convince them they know the whole story.

The situation now contains two people in a conflict based on unverifiable harm they've done to each other. The fourth step is now *pseudo-intellectualism* or *pseudo-moralism*. While Joe is sputtering, claiming that he meant no insult, Patricia is on her moral high horse because she *knows* a racist dog whistle when she hears it, and no one gets to debate whether she's in pain and how much. Her unhealed trauma is in the driver's seat.

Joe, too, claims that he knows how to define a racist, and that's certainly not him! A racist wouldn't voluntarily move into a predominantly Black community, and doesn't that prove he doesn't have a racist bone in his body? Joe has yet to learn that racism is not just an individual attitude.

Patricia and Joe are now entwined in the combative dance of *false binaries*. Each believes they're right, and so the other must be wrong. Neither recognizes that it's good to check ourselves when we are convinced that we can't possibly be wrong.

No one else in the room dares to speak up. Patricia feels alone, isolated, and abandoned. The coworkers she thought she could trust to have her back are silent. They claim to be fighting for justice, yet they're silent when apparently white supremacist ideas erupt in their workplace.

Meanwhile, Joe feels that he's getting falsely accused and no one's coming to his defense. He's scrambling to figure out what to say. If he tries to apologize for causing inadvertent harm, he risks being accused of gaming the system with a faux apology. But if he insists he's done nothing wrong, he risks being accused of avoiding accountability. He's caught in a classic catch-22. He feels embarrassed, ashamed. But most of all he feels hyper-visible, with a spotlight shining on his mistake.

Joe is caught up in the trap of *unforgivability* and *unforgettability*. From now on, when his name is mentioned, a colleague may recall this incident and how he ineptly handled it. The same is true for Patricia too.

The seventh stage is *contamination* and *infection*. Since all hell has broken loose, if any of the bystanders speak up, they risk being accused of enabling Joe's racism or coddling Patricia's hypersensitivity. They'll walk around on eggshells, gossip about this later, and keep their distance from both Joe and Patricia. Perhaps someone will post the incident on social media or Slack, depending on whether they're virtue signaling to prove they're not racist like Joe, or denouncing the organization for failing to protect a Black person from internal racism. Yet doing so will rarely make them feel better about themselves. They know they didn't address an injustice, and that troubles their conscience, another type of agony.

Meanwhile, Joe's coffee has not yet gotten cold.

When Call Outs Don't Work

The Joe and Patricia scenario is obviously an example of a call out that failed to accomplish anything productive. Which isn't surprising. There are five predictable responses to a call out:

1. **Demonize:** You turn the other person into your enemy, resorting to personal attacks on their character, intelligence, and value.
2. **Defend:** You become entrenched in your perspective and insist on the primacy of your view.
3. **Dictate:** You prioritize your perspective on the conflict to the exclusion of how others are experiencing it.
4. **Distract:** You throw curveballs and red herrings that aren't necessarily relevant but allow you to control the conversation.
5. **Deflect:** You take no responsibility, shifting blame to others and covering your role in the conflict.

In short, the result looks just like what I saw in the 1970s: a movement that starts strong but is steadily sliced and diced into smaller groups, each shouting at the others as dissent comes to be viewed as betrayal until all that political power has dissipated into the ether. Then Reagan or Trump or someone worse comes along, and that's all, folks.

What sorts of call outs lead to these negative responses? There are three critical ways in which I've seen call outs tip over the edge to become more destructive than constructive: (1) when calling out becomes a way of asserting ego or power, rather than a larger purpose; (2) when the harm caused by a call out outweighs the harm of the original wrong; and (3) when call outs create a stifled, fearful environment where people are reluctant to engage or get involved.

Beware: When Call Outs Are about Power Rather than Purpose

When I was growing up, I was one of just a handful of Black students at my high school in San Antonio. In the class photos, we looked like pepper on grits. But on the cheerleading team, not a Black face could be found. Each year, all the Black girls were cut during tryouts. And, while no one openly said it was because they were Black, everyone knew. In 1968, fourteen years after *Brown v. Board of Education*, we were still experiencing neo-segregation; it was just more subtle.

I understood then that this was a cruelty and an injustice, but I wasn't going to leave it at that. In response, I created a girls' drill team, arguing that the boys had one, why not the girls? I was the daughter of a military man, and I knew I could run a good drill team using the ROTC training manual. But my actual goal was simpler than that: I wanted revenge.

I made it my personal mission to challenge all the girls who tried out for the drill team. I created elaborate routines with rifle stocks that I knew the Black and Latina girls could pick up without much trouble, but they contained steps and dance moves that would be foreign to any prim Southern belle. So, just as the cheerleading team "happened" to be all white, my drill team "happened" to be all Black and Latina. And that was really all I wanted out of it. I found an outlet where I could establish my *own* power—where I could get my revenge on my terms.

When I look back at the incident now, I see a few different things as I reshuffle these memories. I know that my anger came from a justified place: the decisions made by those cheerleading coaches were *clearly* wrong.

But I also see that *my* response was coming from the wrong place too. Why? Because I was acting out of spite. I wanted to shame and exclude, just as we'd been shamed and excluded, just *because* we'd been shamed and excluded. So, even if my backlash was justified, it only served to further divide my classmates and keep us at odds. It added a second wrong, without addressing the first. It took justified anger but channeled it destructively. It was years before I'd recognized what I'd done as a "wrong"—but that's what I see now when I look back. I see the same dynamic with many call outs today. They stem from a place of real pain and hurt, but they mask the initial hurt, not heal the harm.

"Whatever begins in anger, ends in shame," said Benjamin Franklin, and I proved the truth of that adage. I fell into the trap of doing the right thing the wrong way. I could have embraced the challenge of working with people who were different, modeling inclusiveness for my school, and demonstrating the value of interracial cooperation. Of course, I was only fourteen, so I don't beat myself up for not figuring all of this out at the time. But I can reassess now what I could have done differently and better, so I don't repeat the mistake.

If we're honest with ourselves, I think we all recognize that call outs can come from constructive impulses *and* destructive ones. Call outs that are made simply to assert our own power or to sate our own ego are often destructive decisions—even as they're incredibly tempting. They allow us to embrace malice as a political virtue.

adrienne maree brown summed up the dynamic perfectly when she explained how people use social media to create a public circus of shame:

> We then tear that person or group to shreds in a way that affirms our values. We create memes, reducing someone to the laughing-stock of the Internet that day. We write think-pieces on how we are not like that person, and obviously wouldn't make the same mistakes they have made. We deconstruct them as thinkers, activists, groups, bodies, partners, parents, children—finding all of the contradictions and limitations and shining bright light on them. When we are satisfied that the person or group is destroyed, we move on. Or sometimes we just move on because the next scandal has arrived, the smell of fresh meat overwhelming our interest in finishing the takedown.

It's addictive, isn't it? There's more than a tinge of sadistic entertainment. We get to enjoy the demolition of strangers to whom we never have to be accountable, cherry-picking the bits and pieces of their story that affirm our desire to label them as awful. That's called the fallacy of incomplete evidence, which we use to assure ourselves that we're right and they're wrong. As social media sites encourage the sharpest takes to rise to the top, we compete to see who can react with the most snark. It becomes a form of blood sport, finding targets who are fair game for criticism—for reasons large or small. Celebrities, for instance, because people have a hard time accepting that popular celebrities are not perfect.

Reveling in a culture of fear and brutality does not prepare anyone for the real work of a moral life. These sorts of call outs are verbal violence masquerading as justice work. They're a form of amplified gossip, public indictments that serve to identify to whom people can show contempt, normalizing cruelty without restraint.

When traumatized people feel powerless, they often call out those who have—or have the potential to—hurt them. As columnist David Brooks wrote, "Zealotry is often fueled by people working out their psychological wounds." Given that 64 percent of adults have experienced some form of violence, abuse, or neglect before age eighteen, according to the Centers for Disease Control and Prevention, we should not be surprised when this trauma shows up in our families, workplaces, and communities. Besides, we are traumatized as a country, not just individually—from gun violence, terrorism, climate change, COVID-19, a failing economy, and bitter political partisanship that impairs our ability to build trust with one another. As Ana Marie Cox wrote in a brilliant essay on the percussive impacts of national tragedies, this collective trauma is both underestimated and individualized, as if the coarsening of our political system, inflated wealth disparities, the increase in suicides and opioid deaths, and the explosion in demands for therapy and other coping mechanisms are unrelated. Of course, the damaging impacts of call out culture would be amplified in such conditions.

Black feminist Flo Kennedy once said that "putting your arm around an oppressed person is like hugging a person with a sunburn."

We all tend to see the world through the pain we've had in the past. But just because I've been raped does not mean all men are rapists, even though my feelings of helplessness may be resurrected during conflicts with men. I've experienced racist incidents and micro-aggressions, too many to keep count of, but I strive not to let them determine how I react. I know that unresolved emotions can stimulate my urge to call out and over-punish others. So, while trusting my feelings is important, understanding why I have them is also vital, so that I can make more accurate threat assessments and respond appropriately. I don't care to ruin someone's life (or day) for a sexist or racist comment that I understand is nowhere near equivalent to being raped or killed. It is impossible to exist without being occasionally hurt by something someone says or does—but what you do with that feeling is your responsibility. As writer Cherríe Moraga reminds me, I shouldn't let my past steal my present. We don't have to choose to be offended by everything that irritates us.

It's also important to recognize the difference between abuse and harm. As community organizer Da'Shaun Harrison explained:

> Whereas harm is a one-time act of violence or infliction of pain, that can be either intentional or unintentional, abuse is about a continued and repeated force of violence that mistreats, mishandles, or exploits someone's body, being, and/or feelings. It is about a commitment—interrogated or uninterrogated—to enforcing violence onto someone else with no interest in stopping.

Trauma is real. Harm is real. Feelings stimulated by trauma and harm are real but not necessarily factual. And when discomfort is conflated with threats, victims can become violators through a punishment mentality in which past pain is used to justify the present abuse of others. When we engage in this behavior, we hamper efforts at healing and accountability, embracing instead the disposability politics of the prison industrial complex: punishing, silencing, segregating, and exiling. If these tactics don't reduce crime with all the power of the state behind them, why should we expect them to be effective tools for the human rights movement?

AIDS historian and lesbian activist Sarah Schulman wrote that call out culture is born of an "under-reaction to abuse and overreaction to conflict." People call others out because they feel triggered by conflict (overreacting) but don't recognize their behavior as abuse (underreacting). This overstatement of harm exaggerates our victimization. We end up fearing to upset each other and engage in artificial dances of sensitivities, outsourcing responsibility for our emotional health to everyone else. All of us who wish to be of service to the human rights movement need to attend to our own healing. We should not let our triggers betray our values and our common sense. Nor should we use the movement as our personal therapy space, where normal experiences are pathologized and over-diagnosed in appeals for sympathy. If we overuse words like "trauma," the less effective they become and the less meaning they start to have.

This sort of overprotection prevents the development of resilience. And we end up creating more enemies than allies because we've expanded our definition of who is abusive, bigoted, or traumatic to include anyone we don't like. Failing to distinguish between actual threats and everyday annoyances alienates potential allies and jeopardizes our moral standing as a human rights movement, as everything that discomforts us starts to be interpreted as intentional harm for which we must find someone to blame. Call outs become the proverbial hammer to which everything looks like a nail, and we end up bashing away at opponent and ally alike.

Sometimes a calling out is really an outcry—a demand to be heard and believed. As Paulo Freire wrote in *Pedagogy of the Oppressed*, suffering people can easily oppress others, a dynamic that takes various familiar forms. One version is what I exhibited with my drill team: excluding others because I'd been excluded. Another is the "Oppression Olympics," where individuals undercut one another by claiming that *they* have it hardest. A third is to divide ourselves into smaller and smaller identity groups, trying to find the narrow slice that truly "gets us" while criticizing the rest.

Any movement is susceptible to having our differences—our generations, our races, our genders—pitted against one another. When I taught at Hampshire College, for example, students of color finally—after many years of protests—persuaded the college to establish a multicultural center where they could gather. However, a small sect of Black femme trans students suddenly seized the center, insisting that the presence of anyone who did not share their particular identity would make them feel unsafe.

When asked to intervene, I attempted to point out that excluding other Black students, other trans students, and other students of color was not only immoral but also impractical. To paraphrase Barbara Smith of the Combahee River Collective, which created the concept of identity politics in 1977, we can focus so much on identity that we leave the politics of solidarity on the floor, disused. The students' actions alienated the very people most likely to be supportive. Of course I lost that argument; they didn't seem interested in the safety that comes from wielding power *with* others.

Call out culture treats people as competitors for justice rather than partners capable of uniting for a common goal. It encourages us to become policers of others' behaviors in unconscious service to the politics of domination. And it encourages us to spend our time and energy fleeing for the moral high ground, lest someone else comes around and calls us out in turn.

Beware: When Call Outs Cause More Harm than They Solve

Calling out is a short-term fix, whereas calling in is a long-term remedy. One of the downsides to calling out is that the harm we are trying to stop often simply metastasizes, creating long(er)-term destruction. When call outs become a game of power rather than purpose, any punishment can feel justified—until the scale of punishment quickly exceeds the scale of the initial wrong. We see this dynamic all over modern culture and politics—and it is especially prominent online.

It's a common fear now that one silly tweet can blow up someone's life, even many years after the fact. Because the internet never forgets. Many who would say that "cancel culture" is simply "consequence culture" resist this idea, and it took time for me to come around to it too. But there are now countless examples readily available that prove that cancel culture changes lives for the worse.

Look, for instance, at what happened to Alexi McCammond, a Black woman who resigned as editor-in-chief of *Teen Vogue* in 2021 after decade-old tweets were publicized. She was seventeen when she wrote the tweets, which trafficked in racist and homophobic stereotypes, and she had already apologized profusely for them earlier in her career. Yet more than two years after she'd apologized and deleted the tweets, they continued to stalk her, forcing her resignation. Despite demonstrating empathy and remorse, she was still hung out to dry by her bosses at Condé Nast, who should have known how to handle the situation better.

How many times does a mistake warrant punishment? How long should it follow us around? We have created a cult of unforgivability. Instead, we need to learn the power of forgiveness. How else do people learn and grow?

Or consider the case of a musician named John Roderick, who went viral on Twitter in 2021 after posting a thread about a "teachable moment" he had with his nine-year-old daughter. His daughter was hungry, he said, and he told her to make a can of baked beans. "How?" she asked, and he encouraged her to fiddle with a manual can opener until she figured out how to open the can. Roderick posted the exchange as a humorous "bit," but it came across as cruel. Which made him the "main character" of Twitter that day. Thousands weighed in to accuse him of child abuse. Others went through his backlog of tweets and found several edgy jokes that they screenshotted out of context to provide "proof" that Roderick wasn't just a bad dad but a racist and an antisemite. By the end of the day, Roderick's reputation was in tatters, and he was international news. Dozens of people had called Child Protective Services, and his clients began publicly posting that they would stop doing business with him.

Once the dust settled, it became clear that he'd been exaggerating for effect in his initial posts; his only real wrong was that his jokes hadn't landed. Yet he and his family went through a public flogging.

Living in a call out culture is terrifying. Lapses in judgment from the past can come back to haunt us before we even know them to be lapses because social mores change faster than ingrained habits. This affects older people and younger people alike, as older people are held account-able to rapidly shifting norms and younger people are held accountable for any utterance that ends up on the permanent digital record. What bad decisions that *you* made as a teenager could come back and bite you in the ass now? These "gotcha" moments get people fired, deplatformed, or shunned, without investigating the truth or the fairness of the accusation.

No one can judge the entirety of a person's life story based on the page we come in on. But when we call out others, we are appointing ourselves as judges based on mere snippets of evidence. We demand atonement without ever getting to know the full story. We want instant gratification when we seek accountability; we want abject apologies immediately. And even those we may find lacking if the wrongdoers haven't groveled enough.

Harm can indeed be caused even if that wasn't a person's intent. But intention matters as much as outcomes when we're considering whether to call someone out or call them in. If someone doesn't realize the harm they're doing, there's no point in treating them the same as someone who has acted knowingly and maliciously.

When dealing with friends, we're often more invested in how the other person feels. One of my dearest mentors, Shulamith Koenig, was a native speaker of Hebrew and Yiddish. With English as her third language, she sometimes didn't understand the subtle nuances of English words, and so I winced every time the phrase "you peo-ple" escaped her lips. I attempted to explain to her why this was an inappropriate way to refer to Black people, but she was nearing ninety, so I didn't hold her unfortunate word choice against her. We worked together intimately, fighting for human rights, including the rights of Palestinians. I took my only trip to Israel/Palestine with her. That showed me her heart. So I probably gave her more slack than I'd naturally do with someone whom I'd expect to know better. I was protective of her heart.

When we point out mistakes not to rectify them but to punish others, we seek to shame others, masking a power play as a virtue, as a form of moral grandstanding. But to paraphrase from teaching settings, punishment does not make a bad child good, yet it can make a good child bad. Punishment drives more people away than it attracts, without reducing the likelihood of further harm. Instead of punishing someone or bullying them, we should seek to help people establish new behavior patterns. As Oprah said Maya Angelou told her, when you know better, you'll do better.

Without grace and mercy, asking for accountability is just revenge and punishment. As poet June Jordan wrote, "Sometimes I am the terrorist I must disarm." Why? Because we are all capable of violating others' human rights in the pursuit of justice when we don't practice honest skepticism and question whether we're right.

We should always ask ourselves: What if the people we're calling out are actually innocent? In California in 2020, Emmanuel Cafferty was fired for making the "okay" sign while driving, not knowing that in the wake of the George Floyd murder, that hand sign was associated with white supremacists. That same year, Palestinian immigrant Majdi Wadi nearly lost his catering business in Minneapolis because, unbeknownst to him, his fourteen-year-old daughter sent out antisemitic tweets.

Calling out a stranger online can be a tempting and cathartic distraction, but it is fundamentally a distraction. After all, as journalist Bonny Brooks wrote, it's easier to "burn one person's life to the ground for [a] thought-crime than to organize reform electoral finance laws." We all have more important work to do.

Beware: When Call Outs Create Stifled, Fearful Environments

In 2018, superstar Bette Midler repeated a very unfortunate phrase: "Women are the niggers of the world." The leftist social media world exploded. Then she did it again in 2019, angering the Right this time.

Yes, it was a tone-deaf, racially illiterate phrase from a white woman. But the outrage spent in pillorying #AwkwardBette on social media could have been spent more constructively. It was not only a shallow response but remarkably shortsighted.

Consider how the failure to call Bette *in* may affect her willingness to speak out using her celebrity platform in the future. Midler was trying to say something feminist; she was trying to use her platform to make a point. Her quip was tone-deaf, but her intentions were clear.

We ought to remember that despite the usefulness of celebrity activists, we cannot expect artists to be perfect role models for social justice practices for which they reasonably have not studied as much as they've studied singing or comedy. Artists can reach audiences most social justice activists can't penetrate as they do the cultural work of popularizing our values and ideas. When Beyoncé emblazoned the word "FEMINIST" on a screen during her concerts in 2014, she precipitated a global conversation about the much-maligned word. This was far beyond the reach of thousands of professional feminists, some of whom called her out for coupling her feminism with an unabashed marketable sensuality. But what can we reasonably demand from an entertainer? We should expect Beyoncé to put on a fabulous show, not to have the philosophical chops of bell hooks.

While I'm on the topic of artists, I do want to say a few words about the relationship between the artist and the art, as that's something cancel culture sure has lots of opinions on. An imperfect world produces imperfect artists. Nigerian musician Fela pioneered an entirely new fusion of music called Afrobeat. Thirty years after his death, Afrobeats (plural intended) is now a globally admired genre that pulls together unique futuristic and atavistic influences. Should the fact that Fela reputedly married twenty-seven women in one day persuade us to ignore someone as monumentally influential to African music as Stevie Wonder was to American music? Should his art be shunned because his behaviors were deeply flawed? I say no. The same goes for historical figures. We would always be canceling people retroactively if we used our modern perspectives to extract people from their pasts to judge them. This is called "presentism," where we judge the past through the lens of the present. Everything should be placed in context, not erased, as these contradictions have much to teach us. Art is not just to affirm your point of view but to make you think and sometimes wonder.

Bette Midler and Beyoncé probably won't hesitate to speak up again when the spirit moves them, so I don't think we need to worry about them having been silenced. But the point still stands: any movement that deters would-be members rather than inviting them in is a short-lived one. To punish someone for a mistake without helping them atone or change their behavior is little more than bullying. And few people will be drawn to the human rights movement if we prioritize maligning their character, without offering them a pathway in. I've learned that the pursuit of moral perfectionism can produce more harm than good, and call outs that criticize anything short of perfection are pretentious elitism. This inevitably backfires to create a stifled, fearful environment.

Where do I see these fearful, stifled environments most often these days? As a college professor. I teach brilliant young people every semester how to challenge injustices in our society. I try to spark in them the sense of possibility that I felt in the 1970s when I first got into activism. But they're at a volatile stage. They are trying to orient their moral compasses and figure out their beliefs and goals. But they're also maturing in an environment that is just a smartphone away from viral fame or shame. There's little room to explore themselves or tough social issues without the looming prospect of reproach. And so they're guarded, fearing they will be bitterly criticized when they share their unfolding thoughts. They don't want to be identified as weird, or too different, or anything that makes them attract the unwanted spotlight of mockery.

In his reporting on college campuses, Conor Friedersdorf spoke with a student who confessed that they "probably hold back 90 percent of the things that I want to say due to fear of being called out." After the controversy at Harvard that ended in the resignation of its first Black president, Claudine Gay, only a third of the students reported that they felt comfortable speaking up about controversial issues. My colleague, Smith College professor Carrie Baker, has likewise queried students and found that both conservative and liberal students report self-policing what they say, hiding their true feelings because they are fearful of others' reactions. One of my students woefully confessed, "I can honestly say that I think about getting canceled every day." If students have personal or romantic relationships on campus, messy breakups can lead to overblown charges of toxicity, maliciousness, or manipulation. Others report they are afraid to speak up in classes because they feel they don't have the "right" language to talk about issues important to them.

It's not reasonable to expect everyone to keep up with rapidly changing terminology. Words like "woman," "homeless," or "walk-in" may be viewed by some as outdated or politically incorrect, but many of these words were until recently seen as neutral. And in our quest to find the perfect words, some of our fights appear to defy common sense, reinforcing the perception that the Left is dominated by intolerant "word-policing elites" who are "too sensitive" and out of touch with regular folks. Language policing is sometimes unintelligible even to the people we're trying to support. Psychologist Keith Humphreys suggests that "any claim that specific terms are actively harmful should be viewed as a hypothesis until it is established as fact." Otherwise, it can seem more like a power play than a substantive change in oppressive structures. I'm reminded of a conversation I had with a friend who had recently been imprisoned. When I asked how he was doing, he retorted, "I wasn't incarcerated! I was freedom-impaired!" Language battles should not distract us from the true injustices we face. Don't use your knowledge as a weapon.

"There is an underlying current of fear in my activist communities," cultural studies scholar Frances Lee agrees. "The fear of appearing impure. . . . There's so much wrongdoing in the world that we work to expose. And yet, grace and forgiveness are hard to come by in these circles." It's safer and easier to attack potential allies because of their proximity rather than to confront actual threats. Many students can track their gradual and painful realization about how white supremacist thinking has affected their lives, but they're hesitant to speak out about the issue, fearing they will be ridiculed for their emerging consciousness. Of course, the opposite can be true too. It's not uncommon for someone to learn a new concept and then use this fragment of understanding to weaponize what little they know. I once had a student scold me because she believed that by being on time I'd internalized "white supremacy culture." Hah! One of my students, Rebecca Alvara, wrote that call out culture chills conversations because it's "not an invitation for growth but an expectation that you have already grown."

Students crave meaningful discussions on integrity, morality, and ethics. They want to escape the gilded cage of self-absorption. They want to figure out their values. They want to understand the consequences of their actions and words. But not if they have to be afraid they'll be ostracized permanently for innocent mistakes. Instead of making the world a better place, we sometimes make our movements a miserable place to join. Calling out can make people act against their authentic nature, practicing cruelties they wouldn't have chosen without the peer pressure of wanting to belong. Another one of my students, Margot Audero, wrote that "calling out causes people to think about their reputations. Calling in causes people to think about their integrity."

We are not morally compromised if we talk to people who disagree with us. Choosing to listen to another viewpoint does not signal automatic agreement; it indicates that listening to others matters as much as being heard. It takes courage to engage in conversation with someone who thinks differently than you. Or do we want to only discuss socially safe ideas? To align ourselves with the most popular position? To seek purity of opinions with a ferocity that turns people off? To criticize others' social justice practices while not being critical of our own?

When discussions of character occur in my classroom, instead of jumping out of their seats when class ends, students linger, wanting to extend conversations that were often neglected in high school classes that only focused on quantifiable test scores. But an environment—online or in-person—that's riddled with call outs offers no room for learning. There's no room for trial and error if the first error puts you on trial.

Even those of us who are older and more experienced are susceptible too. One response is to become so fearful of a call out that you're never willing to admit an error. As *Everyday Feminism* writer Hari Ziyad said, "Most of us desire to be 'good people,' and because 'wrong' is so often conflated with 'bad,' being wrong too many times threatens our ability to claim what we so desperately desire to be." Rather than shocking us into change, a call out can send us straight into defense mode, preventing us from listening with an open mind.

People often become defensive when they believe they're being told what to do or think. This is especially true if they are accused of racism, sexism, or bigotry. It rarely works to insist that you know better and that this other person should change according to your wishes. You're basically saying that you do not view them as competent adults. And think about it: if someone knows they've made a mistake, and they know they're going to face a firing squad, they're not gonna want to be held accountable. It ain't gonna happen that way. And so, the whole call out culture contradicts itself because it thwarts its own goal.

If we want to help people reconsider beliefs that we believe are biased, we have to assume the best about them. We can choose to believe that they may be willing to listen to information that challenges the assumptions they've absorbed. We have to realize that their resistance may be a proxy for something else—a sense of being left behind, of not fitting in, of not being taken seriously, or of being bewildered or frightened by the pace of social change. We can be humble and admit we don't know everything that led them to their beliefs. This is our chance to find out.

We also have to accept that we can't change other people. But we can change how we view them. "Constructive kindness is more effective than destructive criticism," wrote author Walter Rhein. Focusing on the positive can lead to everyone's growth, while only focusing on the negative may make everyone feel miserable.

We've all been wrong sometimes, and we'll be wrong again in the future. I've learned that the larger your platform, the more visible your mistakes. That is not a reason for shame. It's a sign that we're not so set in our ways that we're stagnating in our certainty that we know everything we need to know. Taking joy in our curiosity and ability to learn new things is one of life's greatest satisfactions. We can learn to love and trust ourselves to grow from the inevitable mistakes we make. And we can learn to forgive those who gloat because of our mistakes because we know they also are not as perfect as they'd like us to believe.

Some people may be skeptical about calling in. They may think it's passive niceness, a lesson in turning the other cheek, when it's really an organizing practice and a way of life. Calling in is not practicing respectability politics by insisting on civility at the expense of justice. It's not about making minor adjustments to our etiquette so that privileged people feel better about themselves without changing the structures and systems of oppression. It's not inauthentically presenting yourself to seem like less of a threat. It's not about making people feel comfortable in their complicity in human rights violations. Most of all, calling in is not about giving people a pass on accountability. We don't have to suppress our righteous anger or ignore the harm we experience. We can appreciate the strategic use of anger without giving in to meanness or disrespect.

I had to learn how to be more strategic with my righteous anger to create the world I desired and that we deserve. Anger can be a catalyst for change. It can help us understand what is wrong with society and mobilize people to fix it. Writer and activist Audre Lorde famously said that "every woman has a well stocked arsenal of anger potentially useful against those oppressions, personal and institutional, which brought that anger into being." She argued that "focused with precision [anger] can become a powerful source of energy serving progress and change."

Call outs can work when you know someone will never become an ally. But if there is a potential to start or deepen a relationship, give calling in a try instead. It will probably be to your benefit. Few people regret being kind to someone, even if their kindness had previously been abused. And most people want to be responsible with their power, not go around abusing people just because they can get away with it. I try to treat people as if I'm holding the person's heart in my hand and don't want to squeeze too tight.

Besides, too much anger can alienate the people who need to hear us. That's what the next chapter is about, reining in my impulse to call people out so that I didn't sabotage my own goals. After my experiences in local DC politics, I was growing in my skills, if not my confidence. But I had many more lessons to absorb in my hard head before I could make any progress toward the justice I craved.

3.

BE STRATEGIC

A new type of thinking is essential if mankind is to survive and move toward higher levels.

—Albert Einstein

There's a moment of pause, right before a call out comes. A *hush*. A *crackle*.

Maybe you're in an argument, maybe you're on the back foot. But then someone pushes too far. They say something they shouldn't have. They realize it too late. And they stop—mid-sentence.

Hush. Crackle.

I used to love that moment.

Just as it became clear that I would step in, have my say, and take control. It felt like—*power*.

❧

On this particular day, on the other side of this particular pause, is my boss, Ellie Smeal.

It was 1986, and I had been working for her for just over a year, at the National Organization for Women (NOW), where Ellie was president. NOW was the most prominent feminist organization in the country, the authority on women's issues in national politics. But it also had a race problem. It was perceived as treating women of color as the flavor of the month only to neglect us the next.

That's why I'd been hired, to launch NOW's new Women of Color Program. If I'm honest, I was ambivalent about the job. I still didn't call myself a *feminist*, a word that only seemed to describe white women in the 1980s—ones who were middle- or upper-class and always well coiffed, as if they owned stock in Elizabeth Arden. I privately thought that my new colleagues were the women who could afford to burn their expensive bras. The mainstream media's barely veiled contempt for feminism had wiggled into my mind. I used to disclaim the "f" word by frequently saying, "I'm not a feminist, but . . ."

And while I was intrigued by NOW's prestige, I didn't want to serve as a token washerwoman laundering white feminism's image. I wanted to build a truly intersectional feminist movement that reflected the concerns of women of color too, as well as working-class white feminists who were more on the scruffy side like me.

My first year had been rocky. The culture at NOW was cutthroat: closed-door meetings, tight cliques, and brutal election cycles complete with influence campaigns and backstabbing. All of NOW's officers were elected by the group's members, which led to some really ugly inside fights. NOW prepared female candidates for public life and was the political arena in a microcosm. It was hard for me to tell if I was struggling to fit in because of routine infighting or garden-variety racism.

But I'd pushed through, and I was now on the brink of organizing my first major triumph, a first-of-its-kind national conference on women of color and reproductive rights that would bring our issues to national prominence. My friend Donna Brazile was bringing Shirley Chisholm, the first African American woman elected to Congress. After serving seven terms in the US House of Representatives, Chisholm cofounded the National Congress of Black Women in 1984 to assist other Black women running for office. It was a significant achievement to have her speaking at the event.

However, I still needed Ellie's approval for the final budget and lineup.

It was a busy week, so I pulled Ellie aside in the hallway one morning to give her my latest update. I'd figured out the venue, the programming, the headline guests, the logistics, everything. I just needed her green light.

She asked a couple of questions, nodding along until I listed out the panel topics: reproductive freedom, abortion, sterilization abuse . . .

"Wait," she said, snapping to attention. "Sterilization *abuse*?"

I didn't know how to respond. There was a lot I might say.

But Ellie continued: "I had to see *three* doctors and a *psychologist* to get sterilized, even when my husband and I knew we didn't want more kids. If anything, I'd say—"

My face must've discovered a whole new shape by then because she stopped talking.

Hush. Crackle.

Here's what rushed through my head in that pause:

1. That this was exactly what I'd feared throughout the last year—the other shoe, now dropped. That Ellie would hire me but not listen to me. That this pattern was exactly *why*

NOW needed me, but maybe also why they just weren't ready for me yet.

2. That sterilization abuse was one of the most resounding reproductive concerns of women of color. That sterilization abuse was, in fact, why I had started working on reproductive rights in the first place. An early-model IUD had sterilized me a decade earlier after no doctor had thought to tell me about the risks of the defective Dalkon Shield, and after they'd failed to recognize the cause of my pelvic infection as it grew worse and worse.

3. That it made perfect sense to me why a married well-to-do white woman would be encouraged by three doctors and a psychologist to keep having kids. (Hint: it rhymes with *lightness*.) Meanwhile, poor Black women were still receiving hysterectomies like it was a two-for-one special at Applebee's.

4. That this was why Black women still didn't even like to call themselves feminists. Mainstream white feminists only understood their own issues, while blaming women of different races and classes for not seeming to care.

5. And that, at the very least, the *leader* of the country's most important feminist organization—an organization that had pointedly committed to repairing its relationship with women of color—should have one or two of her basic talking points down by now. Or perhaps she'd know how to stop after asking a question and listen for an answer.

Oh. I could have torn her to shreds, torn that whole hallway apart.

But what would I have accomplished if I'd called her out right there?

I wanted our national conference to go ahead. I wanted it to raise the very issues that Ellie had in her blind spot. And I wanted Ellie and NOW behind me, with their prestige.

A call out would've blown up everything. Maybe if it had been thirty years later, I would've been tempted. I would've logged on to Twitter or TikTok and laid into her. I would've found a way to embarrass her or to embarrass myself in the process.

Instead, I rearranged my face and I let that tension fizzle out. I told Ellie that, *yes*, I *did* have some interesting material to share with her on sterilization abuse and how it still posed a problem for women of color.

Then I walked down that hallway, and I exhaled.

Later that week, I flagged Ellie down again, and this time I was ready. I had my numbers on hand, to show her how Black women were twelve times more likely than white women to be sterilized. Intentional sterilization was still rampant in the 1980s. It was the primary way doctors treated Black women for all types of reproductive disorders—just take out the plumbing and then your fibroids, cramps, excessive bleeding, bloating, pimples, swollen feet, aching back, whatever—would go away. Voting rights activist Fannie Lou Hamer was one of the most famous survivors of sterilization abuse; she called it the "Mississippi appendectomy."

I told Ellie my own story, explaining why this was a topic that hit close to home. And I outlined how what we now call medical racism was such a constant concern for many Black mothers like me.

Put in those terms, she could find a way in. She could envision sterilization abuse as part of NOW's agenda. She could green-light the conference and understand how it would fold into her own goals and those of the broader feminist movement—to move all of us forward, together.

What Kind of Power Do You Want to Have?

I like to say that a call in is a call out done with love. But it's also something else. It's a strategic choice.

If I had unloaded my every jumbled thought on Ellie Smeal in that hallway, it would have been a hell of a scene. I would've invented whole new categories of insults, and I would've come out feeling like the victor. I would've shown her just how smart, courageous, and powerful I was.

But I would have walked out that door alone.

I would've lost a potential ally who was powerful too, a real icon in a movement who shared many of my values and championed causes I hold dear. I would've lost access to someone who I *was* able to win over—but only by calling her in instead of calling her out.

I wasn't thinking about it in those terms then, of course. I was frantic and panicked. All I knew was that I was *this* close to launching that conference, and Ellie might be about to nix it over something she didn't understand. Or that I might throw it away if I let my frustration do the talking.

Only in the decades since have I come to understand the trade-off I made that day—by holstering that tempting comeback so I could try again another day. I had to be more motivated by the hope of winning rather than proving Ellie wrong. It was a trade-off between two types of power—one that I knew well and one that I was only just beginning to get a glimpse of.

And perhaps *winning* wasn't what I really wanted. Using language such as "winning," "dominating," and "fighting" suggests exerting power and control over others, rather than a desire for true connection. Did I want to *win* Ellie over or *lean in* closer to her? Could we find our commonalities and shared agenda and not let our different lived experiences get in the way?

Activists like me, in the human rights movement, have a strained relationship with power. Our focus is to combat the abuse of power. When we see someone abusing power *over* us, we fight back. And a call out is one of the few weapons that the powerless have at their disposal to bring the powerful to account. A call out seeks to turn the tables: instead of *you* having power over *me*, I want to shout you down and assert *my* power over *you*. That can work when we're bringing to light the serious wrongs of our real foes.

But most of our daily conflicts *aren't* with outright enemies. We spend most of our time with people who are close to us, and most of our flare-ups are with *them*. We're pissed off at the problematic ally who's on the wrong side of an issue we hold dear, or the family member who has finally gotten on our last nerve, or the coworker who can't keep their foot out of their mouth. We often hold more in common with these people than differences between us. But we sometimes bring the same weapons to the battlefield. I've seen it in every organization I've worked at, and in every family I've gotten to know. We let minor differences distract us from the fights that matter. We lob our best insults at each other.

Why does this happen? When people fear the misuse of power, we often seek to wrest power away from anyone who shows a hint of it. We engage in a form of public shaming I call "punching sideways," instead of punching up at the more powerful, in an example of horizontal hostility. But using our power to monitor and punish others means unilaterally deciding what is wrong. And as Fan Xuan

Chen, a doctoral candidate in psychology at the University of Illinois, observed, the "self-appointed enforcers [who] willingly embrace the job of keeping order" typically "aren't particularly concerned about accidentally punishing innocent people" even though they "consider themselves kind and moral actors." It's a "master's tool" kind of revenge that Audre Lorde warned us about, where we seek our equal opportunity to oppress others.

Even punching up isn't always called for. As organizer Maurice Mitchell warns, we *should* have a healthy skepticism of power used in an unjust way. But this can also lead to reactionary anti-leadership and anti-intellectual posturing. We should remember that it takes years for effective social change work to build collective power in a democratic way.

We should seek to emulate the kind of leadership that Ella Baker, the cofounder of the Student Nonviolent Coordinating Committee (SNCC) in the 1960s, called "servant leadership," leadership that prioritizes the growth, empowerment, and well-being of everyone. Instead of seeking "power *over*" we need to seek "power *with*."

Power itself isn't what we have to fear. We rightly fear the abuse of power. But power is something we need if we want to change unjust situations. And we need to understand that there's a difference between collective power and power through domination. Between the power to build and the power to burn.

When I was young, when I felt the power of that crackle before a call out, I'd fallen in love with power *over*. And I needed to learn that, strategically, power *with* was stronger every time.

Some human rights activists will resist this approach. These are the people who say that we need to burn it all down to be able to build a new society. But if we can't find people to build power with now, how are we going to find them in the ashes?

My encounters with Ellie Smeal over the years would teach me that lesson. They taught me that you could hold back an untimely tirade and be more powerful for it. And that doing so was often simply the smarter, more strategic choice. Because even powerful people aren't necessarily set in their ways or fully formed.

These days, when people sling words of criticism like "performative" or "saviorism," I hear scornful dismissal, not sophistication. Allies can be "proven," "potential," or "problematic." But whatever type they are, the most important thing to remember is that they are *allies*.

No member of a hate group or the MAGA movement ever displayed a Black Lives Matter sign. Or a rainbow Pride flag. So if we refuse to see a person whose front yard boasts a Black Lives Matter sign as a potential ally, we've really shot ourselves in the foot. So what if that's the extent of her involvement in the movement? Let's take that sign as an invitation to reach out and see if she'd like to get more involved.

There is no one perfect way to be an ally, so we need to approach people with the generosity of radical love instead of scorn. We can be politically correct and stunningly ineffective at the same time, losing on policy while we believe we are winning on politics. I'm particularly concerned about the way leftists put each other down for not being "woke" enough, as though this were an effective anti-racist practice. This virtue signaling is just another expression of white supremacy: blaming and shaming are central to that ideology's goal of dividing people and preventing unity across differences.

Of course, there are situations in which people inauthentically co-opt social justice language with no intention of discomforting themselves with actual change. We often see this when a particular cause gets brief attention in the media, only to be quickly forgotten.

This was painfully obvious when the National Football League painted football fields with Black Lives Matter signs while conspiring to keep quarterback Colin Kaepernick from being rehired after he took a knee to protest against police brutality.

But even symbolic gestures provide windows of opportunity if strategically used. We can compel people to live up to their words. As the late congresswoman Barbara Jordan said in 1977, "The people want an America as good as its promise." Work against injustice is often in the gaps between what is promised and what is delivered.

When we attack problematic or unproven allies, we're aiding the oppressors. If we want to *win*, we need to look beyond the fleeting power of the call out and understand how to call in.

Don't Fight a Façade, Connect with the Core

My work in the human rights movement has shown me that many people, with many differing priorities, can move in the same direction toward justice, equality, and peace. There are many pathways to justice—we just need to pick a lane and do the work.

At NOW, I began to reconsider the type of power I was pursuing to try to build something larger and imperfect but hopefully magnificent. As human rights activists, we all bring our imperfect selves to a magnificent cause. In time, I became a kind of "white girl whisperer" within the feminist movement. Over the course of decades, I have sought to bring white women and women of color into coalition, to work together for one another's priorities, even if the conversations get messy along the way.

Why did I choose this role, instead of cutting ties and working harder off on my lonesome or only with women of color?

Throughout my first couple of years at NOW, I kept going back and forth about whether it was worth being a part of the organization. The 1987 national conference on Women of Color and Reproductive Rights eventually did come together, but not without a few more missteps, from me, Ellie, and others. I kept asking myself: Was I more helpful within the mainstream feminist movement or on the outside, trying to build a separate movement for feminists of color? I would seesaw one way and then the next.

But then something clicked between Ellie and me. It was at her birthday celebration in the late 1980s. Her friends and colleagues had all come together to throw Ellie a party, and some brought gag gifts for her. To this day, I do not understand the feminist urge to gift giant dildos. (I think one came from Lily Tomlin.) But each one was met with a giant laugh from the group. Then came another gift that sent a ripple of laughter through Ellie's closest friends.

It was a tiny toy accordion. When Ellie opened it, she looked around and blushed, laughing all the while. I didn't get it though. So I asked her, "Ellie, what is that? Why an accordion?"

I learned that day that Ellie's father had been an immigrant from Italy. When he first moved to Pittsburgh, he was an itinerant street performer, working the street with an accordion to get by.

I was astounded. Ellie appeared to be a cookie-cutter upper-class white woman. Her affect was so pristine that I remember being intimidated when I first met her. Here was someone I had *no* idea how to relate to or connect with. But behind this well-to-do appearance was a background of immigration and poverty. It turned out she had more in common with immigrant women, with poor women, with all of us who'd struggled to scrape by. And the more I talked with Ellie, the more I realized all that had gone into making her who she was. She knew hardship throughout her childhood. But she'd also learned to suppress that story. Because she had to project a flawless competence to be perceived as a leader who could take on Congress, the Supreme Court, and the White House. She'd had to create this image that seemed out of touch with the experiences of poor women. Hell, I'd even seen her name as an answer to a clue on *Jeopardy!*

It was then, strangely, that I realized that an organization like NOW had a place for me. I realized that folks like Ellie and I had enough in common to work together—that we had more in common than we knew how to share.

Me, fighting sterilization abuse, and Ellie, fighting for voluntary sterilization, could be part of the same tent. We each had different, valid experiences that had led us to where we were. And if we pooled those ideas and experiences, the math was simple. We'd be able to reach so many more people than we'd be able to convince individually.

We wouldn't always get along—*no way* would we always get along. But we could work together. And once we did, we'd be stronger together because we'd figured out how to learn from each other. Once the enigma of Ellie began to crack open, it gave me a whole new approach to the work, and it taught me valuable new lessons about dealing with differences in the feminist movement and finding my own place within it.

For one, don't get stuck fighting a façade. Don't focus on the *differences* that leap out to you. You're going to have differences with anyone; that's the beauty of life. But you're also going to have a common core with most people—the values and experiences and concerns that you share.

Start there. Start by digging in and finding what you have in common. Because it then becomes much easier to understand the differences that remain.

This is one of the strategic tenets of calling in: we make more progress if we start from what connects us. For instance, if you're calling in a friend who keeps making insulting jokes, you might take them aside and say, "I know you're a caring person. I've seen you go out of your way to check in with me when I'm down. I've seen you drop everything to help out your friends. So why is there this odd area where you've decided to be okay with putting other people down?" Starting the conversation this way lets them know that you're trying to keep your connection instead of severing it.

Trust is critical, but it's tricky. Many of our call outs or call ins arise with people who we trust partially but not totally, who we agree with on some issues but not all. To navigate these confusing relationships, I've developed what I call the Spheres of Influence model.

Our Spheres of Influence

For the last five years, I've been running calling in workshops online and across the country. After one session in 2020, a participant sent me a story about cranes. She had a friend who was an ecology researcher working to save sandhill cranes in Wisconsin. But the ecologist's projects kept running into issues because the local farmers were shooting the cranes. The birds liked to graze on newly planted seed corn in the fields, which was a disaster for the average farmer.

After several false starts making house calls—or farm calls—to ask the farmers to spare the cranes, the ecologist couldn't help surveying the farmers just as he did the birds. He realized that about 10 percent of the farmers were shooting the cranes because they just didn't like the birds; they didn't want them anywhere nearby, and the ecologist wasn't going to convince them otherwise. On the other end of the spectrum, 10 percent of the farmers thought the cranes were beautiful; they were perfectly willing to go out of their way for the birds so long as the cranes didn't put them out of business. In the middle, however, there was a wide 80 percent who thought the birds were just fine; they could care less as long as their seed corn wasn't getting gobbled up.

In time, the researcher and a team of scientists figured out a neat fix to dissuade the cranes from eating the seed corn. The birds were only drawn to seeds that tasted ripe, so the scientists could coat the corn in an enzyme—easily, simply, organically—that altered the taste. Then, instead of eating the corn, the cranes—to everyone's delight—moved on to eating grubs from the fields, which helped prevent the spread of blight. It was a true win-win. But even so, convincing the farmers was another task.

The ecologist had tried talking to them already; he knew that many didn't want to listen. But to his surprise, he needed to convince only about a tenth of the farmers in that middle 80 percent to try the coated seed corn. Once that happened, there was a cascade effect. Just like any other profession, farmers trusted other farmers. And once they saw the results, they didn't need to be convinced by a roaming scientist. A sliver of that 80 percent improved their crop yields, then passed the trick along to their trusted peers. Sliver by sliver, it kept spreading, until the innovation eventually reached even that intransigent 10 percent. At last, the ecologist—and the cranes—could breathe easy.

This story is an illustration of what I call our "spheres of influence," a key concept for building a call in culture. The ecologist had a good idea—stop killing the cranes—which became a great idea once his team discovered a clever innovation to stop the birds from eating the farmers' crops. But, even then, that change could move only at the "speed of trust," as adrienne maree brown has said. Arriving at a victory sometimes requires we move at a slower pace—the pace of relationships—even when there's urgency. This is something we need to take to heart when we're thinking about whether a call in or a call out is going to accomplish anything meaningful.

It is said that knowledge is social. Since none of us has time to investigate the truth of everything we hear, we evaluate what we believe based on our trust in the messengers: teachers, news outlets, et cetera. (Psychologists call this "epistemic trust": the trust that someone is a reliable source of information, based largely on our sense of the messenger's worldview or perspective.) We believe what we do because of who we trust, and we all have circles of people who we trust more implicitly than others—say, the short list of friends whose music taste remains impeccable, or the sister who can translate what the rest of your siblings *actually* think, or the political thinkers who are either our lodestars or our problematic faves. Each of these people in turn has different spheres of trust and influence, slowly filtering ideas and information throughout society.

This is another reason why we should avoid launching call out broadsides to urge people to lose faith in those they believe. More information doesn't make people change their behavior if they don't think the source of that information has their best interests at heart. If you attack the people they trust, they'll feel like you're attacking them.

In my private theory of change, each of us is surrounded by concentric circles of people we can trust and influence. For instance, I believe that most human rights practitioners—say Ellie Smeal and I—share 90 percent of our worldview with each other. We may disagree on our foci, but we can easily list our points of unity: we fight against neoliberalism, racism, sexism, transphobia, nativism, xenophobia, ableism, and so on. There is always 10 percent disagreement though because we select different priorities and tactics. I might focus on reproductive justice, while someone else might focus on climate change or disability rights. We might use different words or prioritize different strategies, but generally, we perceive each other as progressive allies working to make the world better.

I've spent a lot of time with these 90 percenters over my lifetime, and I've noticed something funny. We spend an enormous amount of energy trying to persuade our 90 percent allies to become 100 percent allies, by arguing again and again over that narrow 10 percent territory of disagreement. Sometimes we fight it out in academic articles or talks on panels; sometimes grievances surface through messy call outs.

Many people mistakenly believe that only perfectly united ideological movements are effective. I'm not precisely sure why people believe this, but it's probably because we're socialized to want simple binaries to help make sense of a complicated world: right/wrong, good/evil, with us/against us. Journalist Amanda Ripley explains that psychologists call this need for simplicity binary splitting. Such binary thinking generates anger and contempt for the "other" side, but it inevitably psychologically harms the person engaging in the "othering" behavior as well. This absolutist approach increases depression and anxiety, as change starts to seem impossible to achieve. Guilt and shame may accompany anger and impatience. And it doesn't help that most Americans are taught a simplified, watered-down version of history so that we don't understand the actual complexities of the struggles of the past.

This all means that we can't accurately identify our allies or our opponents. We don't accept information that contradicts what we already believe. We assume we know everything we need, so we don't question our certainties. And because more nuanced realities can be confusing, frightening, and painful, ambiguity is intolerable and disagreements are exaggerated.

We end up acting as if that remaining 10 percent is the most important thing to hash out, as if once that's done, maybe the movement will spread like wildfire. Maybe *then* we can turn to the task of winning over the rest of the world.

I don't buy this. I don't see perfect ideological unity as a goal that's either achievable or desirable. Our pursuit of a perfect ideology—sacrificing a good outcome for perfect results—is a futile tactic that's characteristic of a narrow imagination. It requires turning people into political clones, not independent, critical thinkers capable of building a multi-issue, multigenerational, intersectional movement.

Instead of ideological unity, I'd rather see us become *strategically* unified. I'd rather see us use our differences as strengths instead of liabilities. To achieve power that builds—power that can win over public opinion and change the system—we must move beyond that 90 percent bubble and out into further circles of influence. Instead of agonizing over that last 10 percent, we can engage with those who have 75 percent or 50 percent agreement with us. They may not know our keywords. They may be repelled by jargon that sounds elitist or half Martian, but they share a sufficiently common worldview, one that values civic engagement, democracy, fairness, community service, justice, and leading by respecting others.

Consider, for example, the Girl Scouts. The organization focuses on girls' empowerment, but it doesn't teach girls about fighting for abortion rights. That's okay with me. I still consider the group my allies—perhaps 75 percent allies. It would be a mistake to insist that any organization I was a part of couldn't work with them because they are not inside my 90 percent bubble on reproductive justice.

The 50 percenters are people like my rather conservative parents, from whom I learned a set of values around family, religion, work ethic, and community service. They volunteered for civic groups like the Girl Scouts and the American Legion and established food programs for homeless people at their church. My convictions led me to more radical social justice groups to get at the root causes of injustice. In other words, my parents distributed food to the hungry while I asked why they were hungry in the first place. When I demonstrated to my parents how their values lived in my work, they recognized that we were taking different paths to the same goals.

Despite our shared family values, we still disagreed on critical issues. For example, I could never persuade my evangelical mother that birth control and abortion were not sins. My mom frequently donated money to Oral Roberts and various televangelists, often to the point where she'd ask for help to pay utility bills afterward. I gritted my teeth in frustration, knowing I was unwillingly subsidizing faith healers. But rational persuasion through love sometimes worked with Mom. When her beloved nephew was dying of AIDS in the early 1980s, she became a surprisingly fierce defender of LGBTQ rights.

My father, meanwhile, was a member of the National Rifle Association and a proud gun owner. He retired from the army after twenty-six years as a weapons specialist, and he took our family to many gatherings at the local VFW (Veterans of Foreign Wars) or NCO (non-commissioned officers) club to hang out with his retired military buddies. We shared a lot of core values, but my parents' religious and militaristic conservatism made them vulnerable to the inducements of those I oppose, which is why I describe them as 50 percenters capable of pivoting right or left.

And so, when I was asked to speak to Dad's American Legion

chapter about a center for human rights education that I was helping to set up, I had to figure out the right language to use to reach an audience that would be turned off by the jargon I sometimes throw around. I wanted to talk *to* them, not *down to* them. So, strategically, I decided to talk about promises kept and promises broken. I talked about how many veterans were denied long-term care at the end of their lives because the government had privatized many of these services. Uncle Sam had reneged on the deal he'd made when they'd enlisted. They understood. I was able to persuade the chapter of the importance of guaranteed human rights by speaking to their values and aligning them with my needs.

Beyond the 50 percenters, I call some opponents either the 25 percent or the 0 percent. They are actually the smallest part of the population, but they have a disproportionate influence because they can persuade large numbers of people to underestimate their threat, making them complicit in their agendas. They are unlikely to listen to progressives because we don't share a common worldview or even a common political language. Their go-to example of liberty might be the right to own an assault weapon or to refuse to wear a mask in a pandemic. We have vastly different definitions of freedom and oppression.

This bottom quartile has worldviews and circles of trust so far from my own that it would seem impossible for me to build bridges only with information and sincerity. People who don't believe in verifiable facts are the most impossible people to argue with. Logic will not persuade them to change their minds because they did not use it to form their opinions in the first place. We can sometimes keep repeating facts until they are taken for granted—this is how the consensus on climate change has grown—but that's a slow process.

When progressives look across this chasm, they often either take it as a challenge to flip their distant 0 percent opponents, or they think there's a simple misunderstanding at the root of the 25 percenters' worldviews that will be easy to correct. But attempts to persuade the people furthest away in political outlook are often futile because we're reaching so far beyond our spheres of influence that we can't build a connection based on trust or even understand which values we share. And, of course, some people are not ill-informed but simply malicious and intentional in their contempt of those who don't agree with them. They cheat because they can't compete. They lie because the truth is their enemy.

In focusing on our opponents, we often neglect those who are closer to us in political perspective. These are the people who we have a real hope of calling in. Our task is to figure out who are the 75 percent and 50 percent people in our lives. Instead of leaving these potential allies standing on the sidelines—or vulnerable to recruitment by those who oppose us—we ought to prioritize paying attention to them. We should not sacrifice them to the hubris of the call out culture and purity politics. Even if these people sometimes call us haughty social gatekeepers or fragile snowflakes, there's still—believe it or not—more in common between us than you might guess. Some will see themselves as liberals, others as conservatives (who despise Trump), and others who perceive themselves as defenders of free speech and unorthodox ideas. And so we must stop seeing them as problems to be solved but as potential allies we can figure out how to work with.

Scholar-activist Keeanga-Yamahtta Taylor warns that call outs "keep the movement tiny and irrelevant." Creating a truly mass "movement necessarily means that it will involve the previously uninitiated—those who are new to activism and organizing." We have to embrace the challenge of finding "common ground with a broad spectrum of people, many of whom we would never otherwise interact with," in the words of organizers Kelly Hayes and Mariame Kaba. It will be uncomfortable at times, but it's worth it.

To find this common ground, we'll need to understand the value of transitional demands instead of all-or-nothing policies.

A "transitional demand" is a partial realization of what you're really aiming for: your optimal demand. It's transitional because it moves the needle toward radical goals to achieve the fundamental changes required for true transformation. For example, if your optimal demand is to end all mass incarceration, a transitional demand may be increased DNA testing to release more innocent people from prison. An optimal demand to end the inflated salaries and bonuses paid to corporate CEOs might produce a transitional demand for stronger unions for better bargaining conditions and to improve wages for workers. An optimal demand to update the US Constitution to twenty-first-century standards might involve transitional demands to enforce voting rights, end gerrymandering, and eliminate the Electoral College in favor of direct democracy. Transitional demands acknowledge that all-or-nothing linear thinking frequently offers no road maps for progress, especially none that are nonviolent.

I sometimes believe that those who most call for a violent revolution have a rather romanticized perception of war. I've had colleagues and icons assassinated. I've been in Nicaragua, the Philippines, El Salvador, and South Africa while those countries were in the middle of violent revolutions, and nothing about them was pretty or romantic. I remember being in Esteli, Nicaragua, with a delegation of American feminists in 1987, while President Reagan was funding the Contras to wage war from across the border with Honduras. I was housed in the home of a Nicaraguan woman whose exterior walls were peppered with bullet holes. When I woke one morning, she was at the stove, frying an egg for my breakfast, tears running down her face. Her son had been killed overnight by the Contras. But she didn't want to neglect her guest, so she started cooking that egg. I despise eggs, but, of course, I choked that egg down.

Transitional demands are an important way to practice nonviolent social change. Let's say our optimal demand is to "defund the police" and to insist these funds be redirected toward actual community priorities. According to the Movement for Black Lives, their data shows that two-thirds of Black Americans support partially divesting from police budgets and investing in areas like health care, education, and housing, while 55 percent of Black Americans support entirely divesting from police departments. Our dilemma is that, despite these facts, the majority of Americans don't agree that defunding the police is a logical demand. We can agree all day over the facts: that the way the police operate does not increase safety (true); that the police target people of color (true); that people of color are overrepresented in prisons (true); that formerly incarcerated people frequently lose their right to vote (true); that bloated police budgets rob communities of vital investments in schools, health care, mental health, and affordable housing (true); and that many of the people we represent in vulnerable communities actually want more police presence, not less (paradoxically true). But if we can't see the necessity of a transitional demand that still includes some form of criminal justice change, we end up appearing unreasonably radical and unapproachably distrustful of the very people whose values are consistent with ours.

Calling in is the practice of synthesis, working across differences and diversities to co-create a new understanding and a new way of being together. When teaching, I frequently cite my favorite self-plagiarism: When many people have different ideas but move in the same direction, that's a movement. When many people have the *same* idea and move in the *same* direction, that's a cult. We are not building the human rights cult but the human rights movement.

This requires learning not to pressure people into *agreeing* with us but learning how to persuade others into *being* with us, keeping a seat at the table, and agreeing not to walk away when we disagree. As Audre Lorde said, "It is not our differences that divide us. It is our inability to recognize, accept, and celebrate those differences."

Saving Our Ammunition

Another thing we have to consider when we sharply disagree with an ally is the price we'll pay by publicly airing that disagreement. Calling out under the wrong circumstances means airing our dirty laundry in public and giving our opponents ammunition to use against us. Of course I've made that mistake too.

While on the campaign trail in 2008, President Obama had signaled his willingness to repeal the Hyde Amendment, a 1976 legislative provision barring the use of federal funds to pay for an abortion except to save the life of the woman, or if the pregnancy arises from incest or rape. The law discriminated against millions of women whose health care was provided by the federal government, including women on Medicaid, women in the military, women in the Peace Corps, federal workers, and Indigenous women whose health care was provided by Indian Health Service.

Like many of Obama's supporters, I hoped he would stand up for women's human rights more decisively than his Democratic predecessors. The next year, however, during the negotiations over the Affordable Care Act, Obama compromised with Republicans, vowing to accept a version of the bill that maintained the Hyde restrictions to secure the votes of conservative Democrats and less ideologically rigid Republicans. When asked by a reporter from the *Washington Times* about my opinion on this disappointing downturn, I glibly quipped, "Obama is like the prom date I had last night who forgot my name the next day."

My smart-ass mouth spouted out words before I realized their political impact. Yes, I needed to let the Obama administration know that millions who voted for him were dismayed by his political calculations. But I didn't need to do so in a newspaper, let alone a right-wing newspaper. That's probably the only reason they wanted a quote from me. I didn't need to load that particular bullet into their guns.

I was amazed to receive an invitation to a Christmas party at the White House the next year. As I look back, I wonder: Was Obama's staff calling me in?

The Power of Showing Up, Not Sitting on the Sidelines

When I was younger, I thought that power crackled right before I shouted someone down. That was power *over*, driving them into submission with a devastating insult. But that's the power that flashes and burns. It's gone before you know it.

When we adopt a strategy of calling in, we build a strategy for winning real power. When we mobilize our spheres of influence to reach our 90 percent allies, our 75 percent allies, even our 50 percenters—that's where the power of movements and coalitions becomes undeniable. Each call in helps build that coalition, like a snowball rolling downhill. While each call out chips away and risks peeling someone off.

I've been on both sides of call outs, plenty of times. And sometimes, even once you think you've won, an errant burst of anger can undermine your best-laid plans. All it takes is one untimely call out when someone puts their personal agenda ahead of the collective one.

In 1997, I was a cofounder of a new feminist collective for women of color, SisterSong, which had been conceptualized by Luz Rodriguez, then director of the Latina Roundtable. SisterSong was a triumph against daunting odds. Organized by sixteen groups representing women of color, it was the fifth attempt to build a national coalition of women of color organizations that worked on reproductive health issues. The previous attempts had failed, mostly due to lack of funding. But SisterSong was different. It was seeded by a three-year, four-million-dollar Ford Foundation grant split among the sixteen groups—the largest grant women of color had ever received from a foundation. SisterSong was also the first attempt to bring pro-choice and pro-life women of color together in the same coalition, along with groups working on issues such as midwifery, HIV/AIDS, abortion rights, abstinence education, teen pregnancy, and health care disparities. Despite the odds, it worked: SisterSong is now nearing its thirtieth anniversary. Our surprising unity was the result of learning to call each other in rather than letting our differences on abortion split us. (I'm sure the lure of the sizable grant provided some glue as well.)

In 2004, after fighting for years to lift our perspectives into the spotlight, a woman of color program officer finally had success in convincing a large foundation to fund a slate of women of color organizations, some within SisterSong and others outside it. It was a crowning achievement, all our labor finally coming to fruition. The final decision to fund the organizations would be discussed at an interracial meeting of leading feminists from around the country, and it seemed like we had all the support we needed. But it wasn't a done deal—the decision would largely be determined by a group of white feminists who, in their minds, were forgoing millions in funding for their own organizations to fund ours.

Because I had worked with many of these white women for decades, I believed they knew that stronger organizations attuned to the needs of feminists of color would benefit the entire women's movement. And we'd made a convincing case.

But then, one of the younger Black attendees decided to stand up and excoriate the group. It was shameful, she said, that it had taken *this* long to finally get a modicum of funding for women of color. White women, she said, weren't doing nearly enough, and even this was, at long last, a weak effort.

She wasn't wrong. But I have never seen a group of white women (some of whom detested each other) close ranks so fast. They felt attacked; they felt their efforts weren't being appreciated. And so they rejected this radical funding redirection.

That was the wrong decision; it was cowardly and weak. But it was also an understandable human response to being shamed and blamed. The call out was all the excuse they needed to maintain the status quo. This is the risk that a poorly timed call out poses—pushing people away and deepening discord.

It's easy to say that the right and righteous response is to draw your line in the sand, not to budge, and never to compromise. But if everyone did that, no one would ever listen to another person's ideas. No one would have the chance to realize that someone in our

50 percent or 75 percent circle might have something to contribute, that they might know something important. You need to be strategic if you're going to get anywhere. You need to open up the flaps of your tent and welcome people inside. You'll be surprised how many people turn out to belong in there—and how limiting it is to be "right" but resigned to watch from the outside.

This was driven home for me in my final project with NOW, which ironically came more than a decade after I'd left the organization.

It was 2003, and I was leading the National Center for Human Rights Education as part of SisterSong. A group of feminist organizations was now planning a March for Freedom of Choice in Washington, DC, the following year. George W. Bush was president, and Republicans had just gained control of the Senate in the 2002 midterms. Abortion rights were in more judicial jeopardy than they'd been in the previous decade, especially as Supreme Court seats would soon open up. The pro-choice movement wanted to make a major showing, to let the Republicans know that they couldn't simply unwind the path of progress. But midway into the march's planning process, NOW and the other organizers realized that they were spiraling toward some familiar trip wires.

They were facing the same problems that I'd tried to help NOW avoid in the 1980s—chiefly, that the march was looking very white. Only a few women of color had organizing roles, and the march was centered on a single issue—abortion—that, while essential, appealed most strongly to white, middle-class feminists. Amid the Patriot Act, increasing poverty, runaway health care costs, global warming, rising debt in the Global South, the invasion of Iraq, and Islamophobia, there was a frightening wealth of other issues that many women of color considered as urgent.

The organizers realized they weren't getting buy-in from many women of color—and they needed it. So, eventually, Ellie Smeal and her lieutenant, Alice Cohan, reached out to me to ask if I could help. Unfortunately for them, their needs were not my priority. I was plenty busy. And I knew from having helped organize abortion rights marches in 1986 and 1989 that it could be a draining task. It was only when Silvia Henriquez, who was then leading the National Latina Institute for Reproductive Health, asked me to reconsider their request that I changed my mind.

This could have been my "I told you so" moment. Hadn't they had enough time to learn by now that you couldn't take women of color for granted?

But then I caught myself. Alice and Ellie had reached out late, but they *had* reached out. Did I want to use my power to gloat and dominate? Or did I want to use my power to build?

I signed on after the SisterSong membership agreed, but we did so strategically. We had a few stipulations.

First, if they were going to fix things, they needed to bring some organizations led by women of color onto the march's steering committee. The National Latina Institute for Reproductive Health (now known as the National Latina Institute for Reproductive Justice) and the Black Women's Health Imperative were added, along with the American Civil Liberties Union (ACLU).

Second, we needed to broaden the set of issues we were marching for. I urged them to name the event the March for Women's Human Rights, but apparently that was an idea whose time hadn't yet come. So we proposed using a name recycled from the 1980s: the March for Women's Lives.

Third, if we wanted a diverse march, then we needed to make sure it wasn't prohibitively expensive for poorer attendees to get there. We needed scholarships to fund trips to the capital, set up through local women's organizations. That was a headache, but we got it done. Not without some squabbling, of course. Yet we got it all done.

The result was exactly what all the organizers had been aiming for: the 2004 March for Women's Lives was the largest protest march in the nation's history up to that point, drawing 1.15 million participants. It broadened the concerns of the women's movement to include not just freedom of choice but effective pre- and postnatal care, proper sex education, the right to plan how we have children, and the right against involuntary sterilization. Many marchers came in solidarity when they saw their priorities reflected the intersectional organizing materials, even though abortion rights were not their primary concern. Taken together, these issues are now called reproductive justice.

The March for Women's Lives would be surpassed in size over a decade later, by the 2017 Women's March to protest Trump's inauguration. That march, too, was a success chiefly because it was the product of calling in tactics.

Early on, the 2017 march organizers were criticized from many sides: by Black activists who noted that the march's original name, the Million Woman March, had been used already for a major march by Black women in the 1990s. The organizers were also criticized by women of color who thought they were being brought into the organizing process too late to help make key decisions. (Sound familiar?) They then faced Jewish critics who laid charges of antisemitism against some of the new women of color leaders who were added. Trans women criticized the symbolic "pink pussy" hats as being non-inclusively "womb-centric," although the hats were created to troll Trump's vulgar "grab 'em by the pussy" remarks. Some of the critiques were absorbed and improved the planning process. Others were the predictable product of trying to bring so many constituencies together. (Yes, that's one of the difficulties inherent to calling in: having to try—and, inevitably, failing—to please everyone.)

But the overall effort to include as many voices as possible was well worth it. Those who stayed on the sideline making call outs missed out on a wondrous confluence of people, best described by human rights activist Rosana Cruz in a Facebook post on January 22, 2017:

> We have it all: half-steppers, disorganizers, unaccountable cookie seekers, the more down than thou, misguided newbies, straight up ignorant fools, glory hogs, cynics, hypocrites, abusers standing right next to the earnest, the weathered, the tired, the I still believers, the I will never be enough, the fire in the belly [because] it has to happen NOW, ingénues, the brave, the brilliant, the I have got your back forever clique, till the last brick falls OGs, strategic geniuses, folks who keep a low profile and keep an eye out for how to build other people's leadership, unsung warriors, leaders and visionaries.

That's the power of calling in. All those spheres of influence overlapped to bring millions of people to more than six hundred locations around the globe, with one voice, making that magnificent coalition heard. The resistance would inspire an unprecedented number of women to successfully run for office in the 2018 midterm elections. That's a prize that only calling in can award us.

While the primary focus of this chapter has been on movement building, calling in can also be a strategic choice if you want to find common ground with friends, family, or neighbors. Another story from the 2017 Women's March illustrates how these worlds overlapped for one supporter who found that debating politics with her neighbors was not the right approach.

Juanita Williams, a cofounder of SisterSong, was part of a grandmothers' knitting circle in rural South Carolina. She was the only Black woman in a group of conservative, white Christian women who gathered weekly in a crafting group. As a fervent Christian from New York, Juanita had built strong relationships in South Carolina, culturally bridging the overhyped racial and urban/rural divides that dominate the national news. But when Juanita asked her crafting circle to knit pink pussy hats, the women recoiled, exclaiming, "We can't say *that* word!" These Trump-supporting grandmothers weren't ready to talk about their lady parts in those terms. It wasn't about politics; it was about Southern gentility.

Undeterred, Juanita changed tactics. She started leading them in singing Tom Jones's song "What's New Pussycat?" and they all laughed when they recognized it. She said they knitted two hundred hats for the march while endlessly singing that song!

Of course, sometimes the best way to preserve common ground with those you care about is to decide it's not the right moment to make a statement you suspect will be divisive, even if expressed with love. I was attending a feminist meeting in Madrid when news of the 2003 invasion of Iraq broke. Within hours, thousands of people had congregated at the Plaza Mayor to protest the war in the most raucous, colorful, and peaceful protest I'd ever seen (and I've seen hundreds after living in Washington, DC, for twenty years). I came home eager to talk about it to anyone who would listen. My first audience was my pinochle club. But just as I started to recount my adventures, someone else announced that she had started a yellow ribbon campaign to honor American soldiers. She wanted our club to donate funds. And she wanted us to proudly display ribbons at our homes to indicate our support for the president and the military.

From demonstrations against a war to yellow ribbons to support it—those are the mixed spheres of my life. Much of my time is spent in movement spaces where all we do is talk politics. But an equally important (and often more fun) part is spent with people who don't let politics interfere with their pleasures. Because we never talked about politics, I was surprised to see such strong support for the yellow-ribbon campaign. So I didn't call my pinochle partners out or in. That day, I called the conversation off.

I often think about the world we deserve and don't have. We deserve to live in a society with strong community groups and civic organizations that feed our spirits and help us build bonds with people all over the country and the world. How else will we get to know— and come to care for—people who might never be our allies but with whom we must nevertheless learn to share this one world we've got? I treasure my pinochle club because it reminds me what an absolute joy—and how very important—it can be to spend pleasant hours in the company of people whose values differ so profoundly from my own.

4.

MODEL THE WORLD WE DESIRE

There can be no action on behalf of the good without
a vision of what the good is.

—Justin Lee

I n 1992, my office was practically a bunker. It was designed that way. From the outside, you'd see a nondescript building in Atlanta. Once you entered, however, you needed a special key to access the elevator. Then the lift took you down—not up—to a secure workplace below-ground. Only employees could get in. Only employees were meant to know we were there.

Welcome to the Center for Democratic Renewal (CDR).

It was quite a contrast: the joyously optimistic name and the lock-down security measures. But it made sense once you learned that CDR was the successor to the National Anti-Klan Network. When it launched in 1979 after the assassination of five anti-Klan protestors in Greensboro, North Carolina, the National Anti-Klan Network was the first anti-hate organization of its kind. Founded by Rev. C.T. Vivian, the longtime adviser to Martin Luther King Jr., the organization monitored white supremacist sects and sought to stunt their growth. But as the Klan branched out in the 1980s into a web of groups like the Aryan Nations and the Order, Vivian's operation needed to expand its purview. And, because one of Vivian's previous homes had been firebombed, the organization also needed to go underground. Hence our drab bunker with its joyous name.

I joined the Center for Democratic Renewal as its program director in 1990. It was a new arena for me; I'd spent almost two decades fighting for women's rights and reproductive rights, but I knew almost nothing about civil rights activism. Luckily, CDR's research director, Leonard Zeskind, and its executive director, Danny Levitas, proved to be world-class mentors. I gamely spent my first couple of years learning on the job, jetting around the country, dropping in on public Klan gatherings, and assisting communities in the aftermath of hate crimes or white supremacist demonstrations.

Fieldwork, however, wasn't exactly my strong suit. Picture a three-hundred-pound Black woman at a Klan rally. I was as stealthy as fireworks. So, I spent my fair share of time at the bunker, organizing anti-hate activists and drumming up resources for hate-group defectors.

One day in the summer of 1992, I was alone at the office, wrapping up work, when the general phone line rang. The voice on the other end was deep and booming.

"I want to talk to Leonard," it said.

"Who's calling?" I asked.

Lenny wasn't in, and we screened all calls anyway: none of us needed Klan lackeys harassing us day and night.

"Floyd Cochran," the voice said.

My breath stopped. "*The* Floyd Cochran?"

A pause.

"Yes."

This wasn't a skinhead lackey. It was top brass.

Floyd Cochran was the spokesperson for the Aryan Nations, the largest neo-Nazi organization in the country. The group had been connected to targeted killings and bombings nationwide, and its head-quarters in Idaho was a hub for white supremacist rallies. The Aryan Nations had also recently begun an aggressive youth-recruitment campaign, and Floyd Cochran was the man behind the push. He had a knack for repackaging Nazi ideology into slick propaganda, to the point where the group's leader had labeled him "the next Goebbels."

On the line, I braced for a death threat or a string of slurs. But neither came.

Instead, Cochran asked for help. He was leaving the Aryan Nations, he said, and he didn't know where else to turn. I took down his number and immediately called Lenny.

Over the coming months, Lenny and I would get to know Floyd Cochran better than we thought possible. Lenny reached out first, to debrief Cochran and gather intelligence about any active threats. Then he handed Floyd over to me, for the human side of things. The man had been a raging white supremacist for twenty years; now it was up to me to guide him out of netherworld thinking.

It was a strange pairing. By Floyd's own account, I was the first Black person with whom he'd held a real conversation. And I had certainly never planned to get buddy-buddy with Nazis—current or former.

But Floyd and I would learn a tremendous amount from each other. Lenny and I didn't have the words for it then, but we were on a monthslong quest now to call in Floyd Cochran.

If my work with Prisoners Against Rape taught me the *possibility* of calling in; if my experience in the women's movement taught me the *strategic power* of calling in; then my time with Floyd Cochran and CDR would teach me the *philosophical importance*.

I learned three critical lessons about calling in from Floyd, and all three were undergirded by a fundamental truth I carry with me to this day: if you want to accomplish anything of import, you need a positive vision. That's true as an organizer, a leader, or an ally; as a partner, a friend, or a parent. It's true any time you want to inspire someone with your plans or needs or any time you're steering through tension or conflict. I've seen so many great organizations break down because they were great at poking holes but bad at filling them. And I've seen shout-downs and criticism win pyrrhic victories only to create environments of fear, shame, and demotivation.

I've organized my philosophy of calling in expressly to replace those fearful environments with ones of joy, growth, and fellowship. It's been my pathway to inner peace and better self-care; it boosts my self-esteem and makes me less vulnerable to my insecurities. Now, disagreements don't mean I'm in jeopardy. I judge myself less harshly, and I can more easily offer grace to others, even those who hurt me and others. My instinct for self-protection is more finely honed, so I don't have to push people away. It helps me avoid negative spirals of criticism and counter-criticism that arouse fears of rejection that become self-fulfilling prophecies.

I've embraced calling in because it's a rare tool that can build rather than break. It helps me understand other people's negativity so that I don't reactivate my own trauma. Instead, I call on my better self to see others with all the compassion I can muster. That's the chief lesson I learned during my time at the Center for Democratic Renewal: in all our work, even the hard parts, we must model the world we desire.

"When You Ask Someone to Change . . ."— *Value Growth Over Punishment*

In the months following Floyd Cochran's cold call, Leonard Zeskind and I unspooled his story. We learned that Cochran had grown up in upstate New York, in a rural, nearly all-white town. He was a stick-thin child, poor and poorly dressed, who was picked on at school and beaten at home for good measure. By his telling, Floyd was an unexceptional kid who would simply have been happy to be ignored. Then, in middle school, he began reading about the history of World War II and the Third Reich.

Hitler was a role model for him, a figure who was forbidden but also electrifying. Hitler was "white trash like me," Floyd said, but white trash who had seized power. And when Floyd, at age fourteen, began flirting with Nazi rhetoric, he discovered it also gave *him* power. When Cochran quoted Hitler, he got a reaction. Kids around him quieted down. His teachers hurried to correct him. Floyd realized he could spark fear and anger at will—and that felt better than getting the tar kicked out of him.

All of this was twenty years before I met Cochran. Soon after high school, he joined the Klan. He'd gotten married and had two sons, though the marriage inevitably ended. It turned out his ex-wife wasn't interested in being a part of a hate group. But that wasn't enough to stop Cochran. After kicking around as a farm laborer, he traveled out west for an Aryan Nations' annual congress—and he didn't come back.

Floyd had nothing outside the hate group; he was milking cows and mucking stables. But within the Aryan Nations, he found a setting where he could feel important. He could be a member of a supposedly "master race"; he could plan for an "imminent" race war; he could explain his hidden ideology to other lost white boys and watch the gears turn. After joining the organization, Floyd found he had a gift for recruitment. He had stumbled down his path to white supremacy, and now he learned how to nudge others down theirs, spinning hateful ideas into alluring invitations.

It all worked for Cochran for a while. He rose to become the fifth-ranking leader of the Aryan Nations by 1992. But by the time I met him, he was questioning his bearings.

Floyd told me that the triggering incident was a conversation with a fellow Nazi at a Hitler Youth Festival. Cochran had mentioned that his youngest son, then four, needed to get an operation to repair his cleft palate. A fellow Nazi told Floyd that surgery was a mistake: Floyd's son was a "genetic defect," the man said. The boy needed to be euthanized, not treated.

Floyd was shaken by the encounter, and he held enough clout in the Aryan Nations that he could go straight to its cultish leader, Richard Butler, with his questions. Was it true that his son should die? he asked. Butler didn't answer Cochran's question, only smiled. And when Cochran raised it again a few weeks later, Butler had him escorted off the compound. A Floyd Cochran who could think wasn't Aryan material anymore.

Cochran was left at the side of the road: homeless, jobless, rudderless. He didn't know what would come next. That's when he called CDR. He realized he'd given his life over to a lie, but he didn't know how to fix things.

Floyd's was a good story. It was a sob story. If I'm honest, though, when I first heard it, I didn't care. It sounded less like tragedy and more like karma. Man plays with fire, gets burned. What else could he expect?

By the time Cochran called, I had been working at CDR for about two years, so I should have been used to meeting people like him. I should have been used to the fact that I'd signed up to help them get out of hate groups like the Aryan Nations. But in truth, I was struggling.

Part of my work was to operate a kind of "underground railroad" for defecting white supremacists. Once they left groups like the Ku Klux Klan or Aryan Nations, they became targets; they were traitors whom their former compatriots sought out to attack or even kill. So, I worked with a network of churches and aid organizations to help defectors go into hiding, find new jobs, and start new lives.

Every couple of weeks, however, I'd catch myself asking *why*. There were a lot of people suffering in the world. Why was I working to help *these* people? A couple of months earlier, any of them would have wished me dead, and some would've been bold enough to pull the trigger. Had they really transformed into upstanding citizens in such a short time? And was this really the best use of the CDR's time and resources?

Floyd's call triggered a new cascade of frustration in me. This was a guy who was so high-ranking that he must have blood on his hands, and I resented being involved.

I didn't realize it at the time, but I was nursing my unacknowledged anger. For a Black woman in America, there are very few unquestioned perks and one of the few is that you can safely and publicly hate a Klansman. They hate me; they're very open about that. I'd long ago decided that I would hate them in turn. It was a guilt-free indulgence, as far as I was concerned. Whatever fate befell them, I did not have to care.

The only problem was that my job at the CDR was, essentially, to care. And, before I knew it, I'd picked a fight with Lenny over whether we should stop talking to defectors like Cochran and focus elsewhere. Maybe increase our outreach to schools and community groups. I didn't know what exactly. I just knew that helping ex-Nazis felt like expending emotional labor on the decidedly undeserving. I pissed off Lenny and myself, and in the aftermath, I went to see Rev. C.T. Vivian, the founder of the center. He was the moral anchor of the organization, and I needed his advice.

C.T. lived with his wife, Octavia, in Atlanta in a large, spacious house on a hill. Visitors didn't have to make an appointment to see him; I'd been invited to drop in whenever I wanted to. He always answered the door, impeccably dressed in a suit, even if it was early in the morning, and he always welcomed me in with a big smile as if he'd been waiting all day for me.

The house was filled with movement memorabilia from the past seventy years: posters of the massive marches he'd been in, awards he'd received, and unpublished photos of legends like Dr. Martin Luther King Jr. He was also a museum-quality art collector. When I first visited him, I envied his original Elizabeth Catlett painting because I used to have a numbered screen print. But his pride and joy was his library. All his life he had collected first editions of famous Black authors. I remember sitting in his library and holding original books by Frederick Douglass and Phillis Wheatley, both autographed. I can only imagine his pain when his previous home had been firebombed.

C.T. and Octavia—who wrote the only authorized biography of her best friend, Coretta Scott King—always insisted we use their first names. C.T. called most young people "sister" or "brother." Although he rarely forgot a face, he never remembered anyone's name who was younger than sixty.

I imagined that C.T. must struggle with his conscience like I did. He had devoted his life to civil rights. He had been attacked; his friends had been assassinated; and, *still*, he was in an endless fight for justice.

That day, we were sitting on the large green sofa in the den. The formal living room was never used, as far as I could tell. I was expecting a sympathetic ear, but C.T. didn't waver when I raised my worries.

"Loretta," he said, "you go around the country telling people to give up hate." It was a tough job, he acknowledged. But he asked me if I'd thought much about what it was like to hear our message from within a hate group like the Aryan Nations, even if it was a potential defector who was listening. From their perspective, we were asking them to give up *life as they knew it*—to break ties, to go off alone, to put life and limb at risk.

"Think about that," C.T. said. "When you ask someone to give up hate, you need to be there for them when they do."

At the time, I didn't fully absorb what C.T. was telling me. I remember leaving his house feeling frustrated because I couldn't cuss a preacher out.

But in hindsight, I see that he was outlining a philosophy that would become central to my work and to the idea of calling in.

Punishment and purges might feel righteous, but that impulse doesn't accomplish anything meaningful or moral. In a call out culture, disagreements are often hardened by scorn and contempt, genuine persuasion is beyond rare, and change is the result of herculean individual effort.

C.T. was trying to show me that I was leaving a door locked in my heart. I was going about my work as if change was impossible—as if mistakes were set in stone, and it was a fool's errand to learn from them. C.T. was telling me the opposite: we *do* live in a world where messy people make mistakes, and we *do* live in a world where some people want to make up for those mistakes. How we handle their mistakes (and our own) can build trust by exposing and allowing us to treasure vulnerability and human fallibility. What's more, C.T. was saying that *if* we ever want people to admit to those mistakes and do better, we need to create room for growth.

No one can change without room to grow.

C.T. had realized this before I was born, and he had organized his whole life around it. He organized the first interracial restaurant desegregation campaign in Peoria, Illinois, in 1947, more than a dozen years before the more famous 1960 sit-in in Greensboro, North Carolina. If we were serious about trying to fight hate, he knew we needed to offer a path out. He saw that hate group members quickly became trapped: they'd often broken off contact with family and friends; they were practically unemployable once they got out (those fully absorbed by the movement don't have résumés); and they would be hunted as traitors when they tried. Even if they wanted to leave, how would they? If C.T. was intent on using a stick instead of a carrot, no one would ever cross over.

Our organization's original name was the National Anti-Klan Network. But Anti-Klan sounds like it's fully against something, and that wasn't C.T.'s philosophy. It was part of why he led the name change to the Center for Democratic Renewal: so we could fight *for* something and not just *against* hate.

I hadn't recognized the importance of that name when I signed on. I still didn't understand C.T.'s wisdom until I went back to work and went on tour with Floyd.

Only the promise of growth could get people out. So, we needed to be there for them—even the worst of the worst—when they finally decided to give up hate.

"Break Up with Shame"—Value Kindness Over Humiliation

Here's the thing that annoyed me most about my work with the Center for Democratic Renewal: it wouldn't let me hold on to hate. Every time I worked with a defected white supremacist I reached a point where I just couldn't hate them anymore. Such was the case with Floyd Cochran. I told myself I would just go in and do my job; I gave myself license to quietly seethe. But the more I learned, the more my hate evaporated away.

From our first conversation, the thing that struck me about Floyd was how bright he was. Before I worked at CDR, I'd assumed that, in a pinch, most Klansmen or neo-Nazis could blame their crimes on utter stupidity. Not so with Cochran. He was lucid and reflective when we spoke. When I asked him about the Aryan Nations, he walked me through his mistakes. He was self-conscious about how long it had taken him to realize that he'd signed on to a murderous cult. And he was candid about how his actions haunted him, even connecting the dots between specific extremists he'd recruited and the eventual hate crimes they'd committed.

For example, Floyd had recruited into the Aryan Nations two alienated brothers named David and Bryan Freeman—sixteen and seventeen years old—in Allentown, Pennsylvania. These kids, enraptured by the ephemeral power of Nazism, turned on their religious, middle-class family. One night in February 1995, they and their cousin murdered their mother, father, and little brother. I had spoken to their mother, Brenda Freeman, only two days before this tragedy when she called CDR, frightened about what her wayward, Nazi-tattooed sons could do. She didn't want to kick them out of the house and change the locks as I advised. She didn't want to make them homeless.

When I asked Floyd how he'd gone so far, his answers took him down rabbit holes. It was as if a whole part of his mind had been turned off for years, and, when he searched for his reasons, he found himself back in his teenage years. Back then, he'd felt stunted at school, unwanted at home, and alone everywhere. I was surprised to hear that many of his root explanations amounted to *feelings*, not reasons. And I was also surprised by the feeling that was conspicuously absent: *hate*.

It hadn't started as hate for Floyd. That was strange for me to hear. He'd never even met a Black person or a Jew before joining the Nazis—he couldn't even find one to hate. Yet when the KKK and then the Aryan Nations swept in, they still managed to strike a nerve because his fears led to hate, and that severed his connection to the rest of humanity. Floyd threw himself behind the first movement that offered him easy power and purpose. They told him he was important and that his life had great meaning. They offered him significance, along with a scapegoat to blame for all those years of angst. And that was enough for him to cling to, with white knuckles, until he simply couldn't any longer. Although if Richard Butler hadn't kicked him off the compound, it's possible Floyd might have stayed, despite his doubts. It wasn't like he had anywhere else to go.

What he did was wrong—that was obvious. But, after a few weeks of talking, it also felt like something I could begin to understand. And after I heard it from Floyd, I began to notice similar stories from other defectors. The press always called it hate because that's what it became. But it often seemed to start as something else: shame, fear, alienation, anger. Then it got whipped up into violence when nothing more galvanizing came along. CDR wrote a handbook, *When Hate Groups Come to Town*, to offer communities advice on how to respond with nonviolent strategies before things got that far.

In response to what I learned from Floyd Cochran and other former white supremacists, I developed a concept called "Appropriate Whiteness" that I started offering in anti-hate trainings. Many white people I talked with—especially poor white people—didn't see a way of exhibiting any pride in their backgrounds without embracing the ideas of white supremacy. Hate groups were the only organizations speaking to this need. I wanted to offer a better option between curled-up shame and reactionary violence.

In my Appropriate Whiteness trainings, I encourage people to "break up with shame," a phrase I borrow from writer Sonya Renee Taylor, who also invented the concept of Calling On. Whereas guilt is defined as feeling bad about something you've done, as trans writer Kai Cheng Thom explains, shame is feeling bad about who you are.

Structural shame is based on things beyond your control. Everyone is socialized into a racial hierarchy that dictates power relations, which in turn dictate economic and social relations. We are trained to live out racialized scripts—but even then, we have choices. We can reject those scripts and self-determine how we want to live in the world.

I do not believe that the majority of people defined as white believe in or want to continue white supremacist thinking. White supremacy is an ideology; whiteness is merely an identity. Obviously, not all white people are white supremacists, and sadly, not all white supremacists are white. That distinction matters. I want to welcome white people into the movement to combat ideological white supremacy; but if they felt ashamed about their white identities, they were immobilized. They did not know how to elevate their joy in being white over their shame in being white, which is probably a legacy of whiteness studies. I needed to let them know that there was room for them in the broader fight—that they could break up with shame without denouncing a part of themselves they had no control over anyway.

Once they did, they could repurpose their white identities for good. For example, when two Black men were racially profiled and arrested at a tony Philadelphia Starbucks in 2018 while waiting for a business meeting, a white woman whipped out her phone to document the injustice, knowing her white privilege would likely protect her. That's repurposing whiteness to oppose white supremacy. It's learning to take pride in being who you are without fulfilling the dominant racial role the social hierarchy has assigned you. A "Karen" would be the opposite of this woman who showed instinctive human solidarity, because a Karen revels in and exploits her white identity. It was probably a Karen who called the police in the first place.

Approximately 45 percent of the white American public rejects ideological whiteness. Where do I get these numbers? From voting patterns. In the 2020 elections, while Trump won 58 percent of the white vote, Biden won the election because—for the first time—there was a decisive split in the white demographic based on age and gender. Young voters were the decisive difference: 60 percent of young voters between eighteen and twenty-nine voted for Biden. White women also tipped left, with 57 percent voting for Biden. Those numbers, coupled with the Black vote, tumbled Trump out of office. (The January 6 insurrectionists rioted not because white votes *weren't* counted but because Black votes *were*.) These anti-Trump white voters are the 50 percent to 90 percent white people who have already decided to break with ideological white supremacy, so it would be illogical for human rights activists to ignore this momentum shift and how it works to our advantage, especially in this inflection point in our fragile democracy. By the middle of the twenty-first century, white people will become the largest minority among a nation of minorities.

Of course, we need to think about the other 55 percent of white Americans too. Many white men today feel they are held to a double standard and criticized for saying or doing things that others get away with. They feel their legitimate concerns are dismissed simply because of who they are. When people feel their concerns are ignored, it's logical for them to become angry, especially as men in our society are socialized to respond to emotional difficulty with anger. We need to figure out how to have serious conversations about these men's grievances without blaming and shaming. Competitive victimhood is a trap. When we try to call in such men, we must be respectful of the life experiences that have caused them to believe what they do. Rather than labeling them with inaccurate stereotypes, we must listen to what they have to say.

Psychologist Adam Grant has said that many of us live in a personal echo chamber where few people disagree with us, which makes us intolerant of anything that doesn't match our opinions. He advises us to intentionally seek out diverse perspectives both in real life and on the internet. If we have debates and discussions with others, we strengthen our abilities to defend our points of view and learn things we may not have considered. Instead of closing our minds to different information, we may perhaps reveal some blind spots. At the least, we'll improve our listening skills and recognize that there's lots more to learn. A church I used to attend had a saying on the wall: "A mind, like a parachute, only functions when it's opened."

In my calling in classes, I've seen resistance by people of color when witnessing white people working on their internalized racism. Some say they feel involuntarily recruited to do emotional labor. I certainly understand these emotions. That's why calling in must be a voluntary act, not an obligation. If you are still working on healing from the wounds of white supremacy, you are not likely to want to help people who are the symbols of those who hurt you. And that's okay. It's more than okay because your priority is to see to your own healing.

There is another consideration, however. I love doing this work because I know I'm part of an eternal chain of freedom that stretches back toward my ancestors and forward to my descendants. I see it as my responsibility to ensure that the chain does not break at my link. (I learned this concept from prison abolitionist Deborah Small after we watched the movie *13th* about how this constitutional amendment engorged the prison industrial complex by allowing the enslavement of people convicted of crimes.) This means that I have the privilege of saying things to white people—with love—that would have gotten my parents and grandparents lynched for being "disrespectful." I cannot walk away from this responsibility without dishonoring those who came before me or disappointing those who come after. It's a matter of dignity, honor, and integrity.

And there's a logic to it. If white supremacy could have been defeated only by people of color, it would be long gone. The human rights movement requires white people who are committed to justice and freedom for everyone. They bring a very specialized knowledge to the struggle because they intimately know what it means to be socialized to perform a white domination role. No matter how much a non-white person studies or experiences, we will never have that knowledge lodged in our bones the way I feel the roots of Africa in mine. They created this deadly system, and they will help us deconstruct it—not by leading, but as co-conspirators.

I enjoy fighting white supremacy because I'm not doing it from a place of anger. That doesn't mean that people don't get on my nerves—but unfortunately, that's not dependent on a person's race or gender. What it means is that when I feel that surge of anger welling up, I call myself in first, so that I present the Loretta I can be proud of instead of the Loretta I can't look at in the mirror without shame. I've witnessed plenty of well-meaning activists mess this up—with call outs that are demeaning and humiliating or anti-racist trainings that brutalize people into thinking that obeisance and groveling are the pathways to justice. But that's flat-out wrong.

This is the second crucial lesson I learned from my work at CDR. Even when such brutal methods avoid creating division and backlash, they demotivate people from getting involved. And we need everyone fighting injustice. Our 0 percent opponents are out there recruiting—just look at Floyd Cochran. If we don't create an entry point, those enemies of human rights will. Worse, if we cause shame and pain, our opponents will sweep in and use that as a recruitment perk.

"Kindness is a language which the deaf can hear and the blind can see," Mark Twain reportedly said. Calling in means selecting kind practices. We *can* make everyone who comes to the movement feel welcome and able to contribute. We *can* inspire people, bringing joy and exuberance by being hopeful and empathetic. We *can* build human connections, solve common problems, and create the beloved community Dr. King wanted, a community based on human rights. But Dr. King's longed-for revolution of values won't come about unless we learn to live differently in ways that actually embody generosity, justice, and peace.

Kindness is not simply being nicer to each other. You can "be nice" and stay quiet in the face of societal, economic, and political injustices. Kindness is political. Sociologist Noël A. Cazenave conceptualizes it not as a benevolent feeling or a generous action but as an ideology. By framing kindness as a universal moral movement, he believes, people can resist "ruthlessly imposing their will on others [and] infringing on basic human rights."

We can all struggle with compassion for others who don't appear deserving of it. When I first witnessed how civil rights activists practiced nonviolence, I didn't think I'd have the emotional control to withstand what they endured. Yet, as I've grown older and hopefully more mature, I understand now that hatred and violence only create more of the same. Compassion is disarming. It showcases the hearts of the oppressed and speaks to the humanity of the oppressors. Compassion and empathy can prevent you from becoming what you despise.

Empathy requires developing your emotional intelligence, as I'll discuss in chapter 5. It also means extending your circle of care to strangers beyond your kith and kin. Feminist philosopher Virginia Held discusses the ethics of caring for others as fundamental to our survival as a species. It is vital for dealing with global problems. And empathy is a skill that can be developed over time, according to psychology professor Jamil Zaki. Empathy is more than feeling another's pain. It also includes "identifying what others feel (cognitive empathy), sharing their emotions (emotional empathy), and wishing to improve their experiences (empathetic concern)," Zaki wrote.

And empathy addresses the widespread loneliness and sadness so many people feel. Writer David Brooks reported: "The percentage of people who say they don't have close friends has increased fourfold since 1990. . . . More than half of all Americans say that no one knows them well. The percentage of high-school students who report 'persistent feelings of sadness or hopelessness' shot up from 26 percent in 2009 to 44 percent in 2021."

Alongside this loneliness epidemic, an epidemic of meanness has eroded our social trust. We exist in a society in which we've forgotten how to be empathetic with one another. Contempt for the unfortunate is distorting our political views and public policies. Laws have been passed to criminalize feeding homeless people, as if common decency is a weakness. Moral education has been so deeply politicized that "Pass It On" commercials by the Foundation for a Better Life run on television in an attempt to teach us how to care for each other. But it's not always this way: I admire how Americans generously respond to natural disasters by reaching out to help without thinking to ask if victims deserved what happened to them. I want us to feel that way in response to man-made tragedies as well.

Calling in is a moral choice to learn and practice the social skills that reflect our ethics and our compassion for each other. We can help each other be in alignment with our belief and faith systems so that there will be almost no distance between who we think we are inside and what we display to others. When we set our moral compass, we understand the *why* of living and not just the *how*, said Holocaust survivor Viktor Frankl, paraphrasing the philosopher Friedrich Nietzsche. This is how you achieve joy and exuberance: it springs from the calm in your soul, the confidence in your choices, and the righteousness of the fight for justice.

"Fighting Hate Should Be Fun"—Value Joy Over Shame

Maya Angelou advised, "We need joy as we need air. We need love as we need water. We need each other as we need the earth we share."

How do we get there? The conclusion I came to after working with Floyd Cochran and other defecting white supremacists was this: *Fighting hate should be fun; it's being a Nazi that sucks!*

That's right: fighting hate should be fun. If you're not having fun, perhaps you're approaching the work the wrong way. This is a lesson Leonard Zeskind taught me.

A lot of activists I've spoken with balk at this idea. We're engaged in work that's serious; it's work that's often frightening and often painful. All of this is true. But we can't take ourselves entirely too seriously and pull everyone else down with our gloom. Especially because when it's going well, it should also be a joy—the most exciting and surprising work in the world.

adrienne maree brown writes that facts, guilt, and shame are limited motivations for creating change, even though those are the primary forces we use in much of our organizing work. She advises that to transform our society, we will need to make justice one of the most pleasurable experiences we can have. brown coined the term "pleasure activism" to represent this vision. Black feminist writer Toni Cade Bambara, likewise, encourages us to "make the revolution irresistible."

This is what calling in seeks to achieve. We seek to replace shame and fear with a sense of joy and purpose. We seek not just to tell people what they can't do, but to show them what they can be a part of. When it all comes together, the experience *is* genuinely thrilling. It's a way of thinking brilliantly together about the possibilities of making a difference in the world. It's a way of advocating for the human right to joy.

Making my life meaningful beyond providing for my family's needs helped me transform my trauma into transcendence and make sense of all that I had been through. I learned that I could survive homelessness, drug addiction, childhood sexual abuse, wars, the assassinations of friends, sterilization abuse, and a host of other tragedies. As civil rights activist Rev. William Barber said about the joy of serving others, "You do it because you've got to take the life you're handed and make a difference with the life you have." Rev. Barber is this generation's spiritual heir to Dr. King, and I like to think that he's a shining example for me—older, disabled, and still determined to share my story of how I keep falling and getting back up.

I learned how resilient I could become in the crucible of struggle. I know I shouldn't have had to endure those things, but I'm proud that I did—and I'm proud that I kept my heart intact. I had some advantages—a strong, loving family; a wonderfully supportive activist community; and teachers who believed in me—and with their aid, I fulfilled the promise I made to scared fifteen-year-old me not to let trauma limit all I could become. And to continue to enjoy the surprisingly simple pleasures of life.

Like the time I spoke to an anti-Klan quilting group in rural Tennessee. The "quilting" was a bit of a front. Their real concern was that their husbands or boyfriends were all members of the Klan. They wanted the Center for Democratic Renewal to come in and talk about anti-hate tactics so they could keep their kids away from extremism and the inevitable crimes such zealotry produces.

I was the go-to person at CDR for that type of work, so I arranged a date and drove up to their small mountaintop village. Traveling alone through the Appalachian Mountains was eerier than I'd imagined. And those women used the phrase "colored girl" like Jim Crow was still alive and kicking. I tensed the first time I heard it—ready to pounce. But I realized it hadn't been lobbed as an insult; they were *trying* to be respectful but had no idea what the right language was. And I could choose not to be offended.

So I made the judgment call to ignore their faux pas and focus on all the things I didn't expect from the gathering. I didn't expect them to be so eager to listen. I didn't expect how we'd be able to land on a common language—one that, for them, focused on keeping their kids out of crime and poverty, but that, for me, served as anti-Klan work.

I didn't get into white supremacist politics with them. They probably knew more about that underworld than I did. And I didn't want to lecture; I wanted a conversation. Mostly, they wanted to hear about my life. It might have been their first opportunity to sit with a Black woman and learn to relate to and trust her. And if they didn't trust me, why would they listen?

Since I'm from the South, it was easy to emphasize my southern drawl as if I was talking to my rural Texas family. When I was growing up, some of my relatives still lived on the family hog farm, delivering a half a hog to their urban relatives like us at slaughtering time.

I spoke about family values—not the kind the religious Right preaches and often doesn't practice, but the authentic ones my parents taught me. Honesty, dignity, looking after family, surviving drinking and drugs. Respect, community service, and bettering ourselves. That was a way to keep their kids safer: giving them values instead of teaching them to resent others.

I listened to their stories of how they joined the white supremacist movement, recruited by family and friends. I told them how I felt when I was eight and my best friend called me "nigger," the first time I had heard that word. I spoke about how a child learns to hate and how it felt to be hated for something I had no control over. I talked about how kids want to be seen as important and how vulnerable they are to being recruited if they don't think their families pay sufficient attention to them.

They could relate to my stories about my dad, who lied about his age to join the army after dropping out of school during the Depression. And my stories about my mom, who birthed me with a midwife on the family kitchen table. Talking to them brought up many memories I'd forgotten. The times we were on welfare, eating government cheese, and stirring peanut butter that you had to remix to use. The way Catholic Charities gave poor families leftover food waste from supermarkets. We had to pick the good stuff from the rotten, but we rarely threw anything away. Cold bologna, mayonnaise, and bread still sound like a welcome childhood meal to me. Hot-water corn bread, cracklings, and pots of beans on Saturdays. All meals that stretched the food dollar to feed a large family. They could relate to that hardscrabble life.

I talked about being a teen mother, something many of them could also understand, and not giving up on your dreams, even if they are delayed. I hadn't graduated college back then, but I told them about my dream to go back after my son graduated. I talked about the power of shame and how it can shackle our hearts and convince us we don't deserve better.

I spoke about neighbors you could trust to look after your kids and not lead them into trouble. Did they want to be those kinds of neighbors? I talked about violence against women and the impact it has on children, even if the children are not directly beaten. I think I channeled a lot of my therapist's words to them.

There were awkward moments, to be sure, like when they asked me to sing a Negro spiritual. I had to decline; it would have ruined the day to hear my scratchy voice. But there were wonderful moments too. I did *not*, for a second, expect to be served the best biscuits and gravy I've ever eaten in my life. There it was though, the unpredictable twist that made the whole day a memory and a surprise. That is the joy of the work.

When human rights activists face some of the worst things people can do to one another, joy is not an indulgence—it's a necessity for survival. We liberate our minds and souls through joy even as our bodies, our lands, and our ways of life are colonized and threatened. The hope and joy I've seen through my work have helped me not give in to despair and cynicism. Those negative feelings make me feel like I've already died before I've even lived. Hope is my fuel for the struggle.

Without hope, activism itself can increase unhappiness. It can provoke anger and hatred toward others and create a toxic win-lose mentality. Historian Howard Zinn also spoke to the necessity of hope for those who wish to create change:

> To be hopeful in bad times is not just foolishly romantic. . . . If we see only the worst, it destroys our capacity to do something. If we remember those times and places—and there are so many— where people have behaved magnificently, this gives us the energy to act. . . . The future is an infinite succession of presents, and to live now as we think human beings should live, in defiance of all that is bad around us, is itself a marvelous victory.

This is the sense of possibility that calling in allows for but that calling out writes off. You should want to be surprised; and you should open the door to surprise—even from people you disagree with. That doesn't mean being reckless; I got the hell off that mountaintop before sundown.

The joy of activism can look like an amazing outpouring of

community solidarity, like when ten thousand menorahs went up around Billings, Montana, in 1994 after someone threw a rock through a Jewish child's window during Hanukkah. But it can also be private and even a bit sly. In the early 1990s, I was tasked with conducting a training on recognizing hate crimes for the FBI. I entered a classroom filled with about thirty men seated at rigid school desks, like the ones for children. Most, if not all, had weapons at their sides. I was nervous because my dreadlocks made me look like a female Jamaican posse member—probably one of their training targets. The agents didn't move their hands more than six inches from their guns as far as I could see. It was unconscious; it was their training.

I knew they might feel threatened by the possibility that someone like me could have something important to teach them. And if they felt threatened, they'd probably just dismiss what I had to say. So when I introduced myself, I deliberately mispronounced a word. I think it was mis-chee'-vi-ous. I intentionally offered this mispronunciation to allow them to correct me and gain the upper hand, thus restoring their sense of control. Within seconds, one guy shouted a correction to put me in my place. I could feel the tension leave the room, and I proceeded with the training. That was probably the most subtle calling in I ever did. And I took great pleasure in knowing that I'd planned it well.

"Where's the Movement?"—Value Fellowship Over Fracture

Working with Floyd eventually brought me to other moments of joy as well. Once he was on his feet and had a place to live, it was time for the interesting work to begin. Floyd truly was a talented speaker who knew the Bible like a preacher and had a deep bass voice that was riveting. He wasn't a fast talker, modulating his pace so his audience could easily keep up. He was eager to redirect those skills against the hateful talking points he'd spouted for the Aryan Nations. I ended up helping to arrange a speaking tour of sorts for him.

Ask me if I ever expected I'd be on tour with a white supremacist, I dare you.

But off we went, across the country. Floyd spoke everywhere from small town meetings to national talk shows like Jerry Springer's. Springer had arranged a confrontation for him with a current neo-Nazi and also invited a Black woman who had lost a child to a hate crime. I was backstage, trying to stay far, far away from whatever fireworks might erupt. But the real excitement was actually the night before. The show was filmed in Chicago, and we had requested an anonymous hotel for security reasons, but it turned out that the logistics person had placed all the guests at the same hotel. While we were eating dinner, Floyd spotted the neo-Nazi in the lobby. We hurriedly finished our meal and retreated to our rooms for the night. Floyd was understandably upset.

Floyd was willing to talk to anyone who would listen about the dangers of white supremacist groups—or about the damage he'd done and how to prevent the lies he'd promoted from reaching the next generation. As we settled into the tour, we got to know each other pretty well. We could joke and bat ideas back and forth. For a long time, I hesitated to admit it, but the trips even became *fun*. He'd regale me with, say, the story of a drunk guy coming to the Idaho compound, shouting he wanted to become a Nazi. Floyd was near the gate, so he saw the guy lift his T-shirt from his enormous beer belly to proudly display a swastika tattooed from his man breasts to his belly button.

If this is a sample of the master race, we're in trouble! Floyd thought to himself.

I mean, it was never a true buddy comedy: Floyd was still struggling to unlearn a lot of ugly ideas—like homophobia—and there's also only so much safety a Black woman can expect in a small, predominantly white town that's fighting a hate group. All of our trips were to the Midwest and the Pacific Northwest, hotbeds of hate group activity. Neo-Nazis and skinheads would choose a bucolic nearly all-white town and start distributing flyers, holding unpermitted demonstrations, and creating a furor, even if there were only three or four of them. Sometimes, anti-racist skinheads, called ARA (Anti-Racist Action), would show up to fight them. I could never relax because I couldn't distinguish who was a safe white person from the kooks. But considering all the dread and frustration I'd had coming into my work with Floyd, our fun was a welcome surprise.

After a few months of traveling from event to event with Floyd, however, I could tell he was getting antsy.

We'd just wrapped up a long event when he turned to me.

"Loretta," he asked, "where's the *movement* I can join?"

"What do you mean?" I said.

"Well, you know I'm a good speaker. And I'm a pretty good recruiter too. I really do want to make up for my past." But he had started to see the media events as a carnival: a lot of flash without much staying power. "Where's the movement?"

Floyd, I realized, wasn't thinking all that differently from me. He was a movement guy at his core. He'd spent all those years recruiting members and motivating them, and he knew that you could organize people to create real change. He'd just been doing it for the wrong cause.

I didn't have a great answer for Floyd at that moment. I knew the women's movement best, but that wasn't what Floyd had in mind. The civil rights movement was the obvious choice, but would an ex-Nazi be welcomed? The most active organizations had also, in recent years, disappeared because of a lack of funding. Even at the Center for Democratic Renewal, our main focus was monitoring and documenting hate groups. Was that a *movement*, exactly?

When I couldn't come up with a good answer, Floyd's question became my question. I couldn't stop thinking about it.

When I got back home, I visited C.T. Vivian again. I told him about Floyd and our conversation: here was someone who now wanted to help, but who didn't know where to sign up, let alone what to join.

C.T. took it all in and looked at me intently. "Did you know," he asked, "that Martin never meant to build a civil rights movement?"

C.T. always called Dr. Martin Luther King Jr. "Martin," a familiarity that never failed to surprise me. But that wasn't why I was now scowling at him like he'd lost his mind.

"He didn't want a civil— What?" I sputtered.

"Martin meant to build a *human* rights movement," he said.

C.T. walked over to his bookshelves and took down a copy of King's last Sunday sermon at the National Cathedral, from March 31, 1968. In it, King spoke about a "triple revolution" that the world was undergoing: a revolution in technology, making it possible to reach almost anywhere on the planet in an instant; a revolution in weaponry, with the arrival of the atomic bomb; and "the human rights revolution, with the freedom explosion that is taking place all over the world." And yet, King said, "One of the great liabilities of life is that all too many people find themselves living amid a great period of social change and yet they fail to develop the new attitudes, the new mental responses—that the new situation demands. They end up sleeping through a revolution."

King argued that, for every person on the planet, the threats and opportunities we were now facing were all connected. "We are tied together in the single garment of destiny," he proclaimed, "caught in an inescapable network of mutuality. And whatever affects one directly affects all indirectly. For some strange reason, I can never be what I ought to be until you are what you ought to be. And you can never be what you ought to be until I am what I ought to be."

King stated, "We have made this world a neighborhood and yet . . . we have not had the ethical commitment to make it a brotherhood."

That, C.T. said, was King's vision—his grand plan. King saw that the civil rights movement in the United States was connected to anti-colonial revolutions in Africa, which were connected to freedom of speech campaigns in China, which were connected to anti-poverty campaigns in India, which were connected to anti-war movements, environmental movements, women's rights movements, anti-discrimination movements, health care movements, et cetera.

It was all one larger movement—a human rights movement—with room for everyone.

When C.T. walked me through that sermon, I must have looked like I'd seen a ghost. I'd known King had a dream, but I didn't realize he had *a plan*. I'd been involved in activism for years, but I didn't know anything about the human rights movement that Dr. King had begun to unveil. "Human rights" was a phrase I connected only with war crimes abroad or the Geneva Convention. I hadn't considered that I, Floyd Cochran, or anyone else, could advocate for human rights here at home.

That conversation with C.T. Vivian transformed my outlook—it offered the final vivid lesson of my work with Floyd Cochran and CDR. C.T. taught me that anybody working for the good of humanity needs a positive vision to motivate them, and he showed me that the human rights movement could provide that vision for anybody working for positive change.

After that conversation, I realized that all the work I had done thus far in my life fit under the umbrella of human rights. And I realized that the human rights movement was the unifying force I'd been looking for. When I'd been in DC, I'd witnessed radical groups spit all their venom at one another, losing sight of their real priorities. They forgot that it's an honor to work for human rights because it's a joy to serve others. Dr. King had seen those divisions in the civil rights movement too—there'd been homophobia, fears of being called communists, and a fight over whether to even support the Universal Declaration of Human Rights. But he'd never gotten the chance to organize his plan to bring human rights home to the United States. He was assassinated only four days later.

Ever since I spoke with C.T., I've made it my life's work to spread the wings of the human rights movement. A couple of years later, a group of us—Shulamith Koenig, Rev. C.T. Vivian, Abdullahi An-Na'im, and I—decided to launch a new organization, the National Center for Human Rights Education (NCHRE). We were a Jew, a Baptist, a Muslim, and a humanist coming together to fulfill Dr. King's dream of bringing human rights home. Our mission was to address the fact that people can't fight for rights they don't know they have. A survey on the fiftieth anniversary of the Universal Declaration of Human Rights in 1998 revealed that only 7 percent of the US public had even heard of the document. Over the next ten years, NCHRE provided human rights education to more than one million people.

Half a century after King's final sermon, his vision of a sweeping human rights revolution remains incomplete. And yet, in the past two decades, a new US human rights movement has emerged, re-envisioned chiefly by women of color. Human rights language is being integrated into social justice movements throughout the country, providing a common framework, language, and goal. As a college professor, I'm now leading an initiative to provide human rights education and calling in techniques to every student who graduates from Smith College. As C.T. predicted, human rights are in everything I do.

Human rights—the basic necessities that a human being needs to survive and to chart a life of their own choosing—offer the clearest statement of our collective values that humanity has created to date. We can use the human rights framework—the ideology, but also the moral standards, the treaties, the laws—to shift peoples' understanding about what society should achieve and how our tax dollars should be used to take care of people's needs.

Since the first settlers arrived on these shores, the United States has been fighting to realize its own ideals. As civil rights scholar Vincent Harding wrote, "We are citizens of a country that does not exist." Each generation has struggled to achieve the promise of America, willing it into existence. Our public health, education, infrastructure, military, criminal justice, and electoral systems are brittle at best; they struggle to withstand the increasing pressures of the twenty-first century.

To prevail, we need to lead a revolution of moral renewal, a revolution that encompasses a vast range of people with a common vision of where we're headed. As Audre Lorde said, we need a vision that is "rooted in human possibility and growth that does not shrivel before adversity," a vision that is resilient, timeless, and capacious enough to hold all our dreams.

Calling in is about choosing our path toward human rights instead of letting the future just happen to us. We will inevitably stumble. But to get back up and move forward, we have to learn to be more forgiving of strangers and more understanding of our allies. It's a matter of morality. It's a matter of strategy. It's a matter of ushering in growth, joy, and fellowship. And it's a matter of modeling the world we desire—so that we can make that world a reality.

When I brought Dr. King's vision of human rights back to Floyd Cochran, it clicked with him as well. The human rights movement could be a big tent, one that could somehow include both an ex-neo-Nazi like him and a Black feminist like me. We could each work in our own lane, apply our own expertise, and lend a hand to allied movements too.

One of the best memories I have is of Floyd working up the courage to speak in favor of an LGBTQ rights antidiscrimination law that was coming up for a vote in Montana. He was nervous because he didn't yet have relationships with LGBTQ people and feared he would get the terminology wrong. But despite how difficult he found it, he stepped up for his allies. I appreciated that he was scared but chose to do the right thing anyway. It's hard to imagine him making that leap if he hadn't made the human rights movement *his* movement.

Those of us who do human rights work are noticing an amazing "justice" alignment happening in the universe: social justice, economic justice, reproductive justice, youth justice, housing justice, food justice, health justice, environmental justice, education justice, sexual justice, racial justice, gender justice, and so on. (Notice that *criminal*

justice is not on this list because there is little that is just about our system of mass incarceration, and even members of the Supreme Court can be bought at bargain-basement prices.) The twenty-first century can begin a millennium of human rights if we go beyond simplistic demands for equality to stitch all of these movements together into an intersectional human rights quilt that foregrounds accountability and achieves justice. We can build a beautifully inclusive global society, created in communities bonded by love and the common goal of the liberation of mind, heart, and spirit. We can connect to Mother Earth and every creature in the universe. The power of numbers will defeat the power of the purse anytime.

But first, we must renew our connections with ourselves.

As Rev. angel Kyodo williams said, "For us to transform as a society, we have to allow ourselves to be transformed as individuals. And for us to be transformed as individuals, we have to allow . . . a real forgiveness for the complexity of human beings."

I believe that the only identity that really matters is our moral identity—who we are in relationship to the truth, to honesty, to compassion, and to others. Calling in is the process of finding out who you really are in the midst of the stress that's compelling you to be someone else, someone less kind and more cruel. It provides moral clarity. It takes courage to be true to your own integrity, especially when there are benefits to doing otherwise. But people unable to love or trust themselves cannot be there for others. If you are ignorant of your foibles and ruled by unseemly passions, you may carelessly destroy someone else's life. We cannot be indifferent to the sufferings of others. And so, we cannot be indifferent to the suffering of ourselves.

Now that we understand why calling in is important, we can learn *how* to call people in, beginning with ourselves.

5.

STARTING WITH THE SELF

Love is that condition in the human spirit so profound that it allows us to forgive.

—Maya Angelou

My screen flooded with one leaden block of text after the next. A squall of italics here. Underline that. THIS LINE NEEDS TO BE ALL CAPS. Should I cc this colleague? Yes. This funder? Yes. Are you sure you want to send this message at 11:57 p.m.? To everyone? *YES!*

It was 2004, and social media was still in its infancy, so I was doing my damnedest to make a fool of myself over email.

I was eight years into my tenure as the head of the National Center for Human Rights Education, and the itch to move on had been growing. For the past few years, NCHRE had been part of a coalition of women of color–led organizations called SisterSong, a collective I'd helped to found. I had just accepted the role as the collective's national coordinator, and I was eager to start off right. I was closing a loop, returning to the type of reproductive justice activism I had helped jump-start earlier in my career—when a dozen of us Black feminists coined the very term "reproductive justice" in 1994. Reproductive justice sought to protect not just the right to abortion but the right to have children and to do so safely. We wanted the right to raise our children in safe and healthy environments; to see them thrive, but not at the expense of ourselves.

So, when a colleague called me to let me know there was another organization—a group of non-Black women of color—making the rounds, saying that *they* had invented the concept of "reproductive justice," it rubbed me wrong. Worse? This group was also a member of the SisterSong collective.

I had a flash of panic. We were already vulnerable to competition from more mainstream organizations for limited funding. If member organizations started trying to cut the national office out of our funding streams, that could harm the collective. And if a non-Black organization falsely claimed credit for something they didn't create, would the past work of Black feminists vanish from the record?

That panic ignited into rage. I opened up an email tab, and I didn't stop typing until I'd set the record straight. My email was directed to the leader of the upstart organization—a young woman I'll call Angela. And for good measure, I cc'd everyone else in the SisterSong collective, along with all the donors and other big players I knew at feminist organizations around the country.

In my email tirade, I laid into Angela. I accused her of blatant "intellectual theft." I questioned her morals. Why would a fellow woman of color steal from her comrades so brazenly? Shouldn't she have known better? Or done a little research? Was she really fit to lead an organization?

It was a take-no-prisoners call out. And the fallout was catastrophic.

Angela was mortified, blindsided, reduced to tears. The bystanders were shocked—not at Angela so much, but at me. And my screed rebounded right back at me in a reply-all firestorm. Karma is a bitch, and she has great aim.

I hadn't stopped for a moment to think about my own power and responsibility. Angela was thirty years younger than me, with thirty years less clout in activist organizations. I hadn't realized it, but I wasn't the underdog. I had a career and a legacy, and the power to threaten Angela's whole career right as it was beginning. I also hadn't stopped to consider approaching her individually, to see if there was more to the story I'd been told, to see if she'd been genuinely unaware of the term's history. Since I was unwilling to question if I was wrong, I didn't do anything right.

Instead, I created a spectacle of blame. I assumed the worst of Angela; I thought she was trying to steal and erase our legacy. So, I gave myself license to become a bully. And I didn't just insult *her*; I blew up a spate of relationships. A few organizations left SisterSong in response, weakening the collective. I pissed off my staff by acting out. I'd unleashed a flood of issues that didn't have to exist. I could have simply had a one-on-one conversation with Angela. I could have called her up and called her in.

Even for me, calling in isn't always easy. Even after I'd put in decades of work as an activist, even after years of promoting the virtues of an empathetic human rights framework, I still could mess it all up in an instant. I still do.

I know my calling in lessons now, inside and out. But to put them into practice takes more than just knowledge. Because I still have an ego. I still get angry, frustrated, and exhausted. I still have years of trauma that flares up unexpectedly. If I'm not careful, whenever stress strikes, my crueler impulses will take the wheel. Good luck, then, to anyone in the vicinity. The firestorm is coming.

This is why I believe that calling in needs to start with the self.

Before you or I seek to counsel or confront someone, we need to make sure that we're in the right place, mentally and emotionally, to do so. Most errant call outs come from a place of anger, insecurity, or hurt. If you or I are going to outsmart those emotions, we need to develop reserves of patience and understanding—not just for others, but for ourselves. Because if we don't heal those bleeding parts of ourselves, we're going to bleed all over others. That's what I did when I called out Angela. I let my anger lead, and it led to disaster.

Anger, Pain, Ego—What Hurts Your Ability to Help?

Anger will always have a purpose in fighting injustice. It can be fueling, even liberatory. We use our anger to bring attention to wrongdoing and to demand amends. We also use anger to survive trauma and to keep pushing from one day to the next. We shouldn't be afraid of our anger, nor should we be chastened into silence when there are justified reasons for outrage.

But anger can also build up, like a static charge, demanding to be released. If we don't channel it to a fitting outlet, our anger will fry us from the inside, or surge without warning. Then, we strike out at the people closest at hand—at our loved ones or whichever poor soul happens to get in our way.

I know anger well. It's an old friend who still keeps a spare set of keys. I used to trust my anger to guide me. In my twenties in DC, I lived on the fumes of indignation. There was always a political cause to throw myself into. But my run-ins with bosses and coworkers created more headaches than they ever needed to, like when I went off on a boss who kept removing my *Washington Post* from my desk. I've probably missed opportunities for advancement because I was perceived as "difficult" to work with. People were afraid of my blunt tactlessness. I was proud of not having a filter—and gee, was I wrong.

My work with Prisoners Against Rape showed me my anger was often misguided and ineffectual.

Then, I had to really reassess after I berated Angela.

Since then, my hard head has begun to absorb a few decades' worth of lessons. I've learned that, as Audre Lorde predicted, my anger doesn't protect me. Anger clouds my thinking and stops me from processing what's going on. It detours me toward visions of revenge and punishment, toward a cathartic call out, where I can release the built-up charge like a lightning bolt. But it takes an obvious toll. It leaves me ragged and on edge, and it turns call out–riven spaces into minefields, where one frustrated outburst sets off the next.

I've had to identify the impulses that get in the way of the work I want to accomplish. And I've determined that I no longer want to be driven chiefly by anger.

At a recent training I ran at Harvard, a participant asked if suppressing anger at white privilege was merely a way of inauthentically engaging in respectability politics to avoid the "angry Black woman" stereotype. And it's true that when I get angry or frustrated, I "lose the room," as they say, because an angry Black woman frightens people, no matter how justified her rage. It's often not what we say or how; people are offended that we've spoken at all. Our comportment is overpoliced by those who believe we don't have the right to the same range of emotions as white people.

But that's not *why* I call myself in.

In response to her question, I asked the participant who she was inside. She said she was filled with love. Which, then, was her authentic self—the person leading with anger or the person leading with love? We all have a choice not to play the roles society forces upon us. We can decide how we'll address injustice while not betraying our good opinion of ourselves. We can choose not to practice cruelties we wouldn't have chosen without the peer pressure of wanting to belong.

If you believe love is who you are, act like it! Cultivate curiosity, forgiveness, patience, empathy, and understanding. It ain't easy, but it's much more difficult to be untrue to your inner values because that always leaves you feeling worse about yourself. Always try to make decisions you can be proud of.

In anti-oppression work, we'll inevitably feel angry, anxious, or hurt at some point. As embodiment facilitator Prentis Hemphill pointed out, "Oppression is . . . basically ensuring that some people will experience pain disproportionately and that, simultaneously, they will lose the resources to heal from the trauma they experience." But anyone working for change needs to be able to channel charged emotions without being overcome by them. Let's learn to be trauma-informed, not trauma-controlled.

I've found that my unavoidable negative emotions—anger, pain, anxiety—can best be countered by love. As Martin Luther King Jr. said, "Power without love is reckless and abusive, and love without power is sentimental and anemic. Power at its best is love implementing the demands of justice, and justice at its best is power correcting everything that stands against love."

King's words have become a North Star to me as I've learned to call myself in.

All those years, when I was acting out of unfocused anger, I've realized I was mostly just *venting*. I could make excuses and tie a bow on it—*Angela* was in the wrong, that prisoner William Fuller should have known better. But ultimately I was acting out to make *myself* feel better, rather than to make my world better.

What do I mean by this? I mean that when I really examined the root causes of my actions, I found that my anger generally wasn't born out of righteousness. It was born out of pain. I might find reasons to say that I was fighting for justice or some other large purpose, but those reasons were just smokescreens. I needed to be honest with myself. Part of learning to be an adult is learning to tell fewer lies to oneself. I needed to realize that there could be a difference between calling out an injustice and calling out in pain.

In "Notes of a Native Son," James Baldwin wrote, "I imagine that one of the reasons people cling to their hates so stubbornly is because they sense, once hate is gone, that they will be forced to deal with pain." What I've learned in my life, one jagged lesson at a time, is that Baldwin is right. Even once I recognized that anger was blocking my thinking, I didn't understand it until I faced the pain underneath.

The intensity and urgency of my anger at Angela had frightened me; I understood the spurt of rage, but not how it had swept me up in its wake. As I went back over it in therapy, I started to see the pressure point that set me off.

The phone call I'd gotten about someone else taking credit for creating reproductive justice hit a wound that I wasn't aware of. If you've read this far, you know I have a history of trauma going all the way back to childhood. As an adult, I had come to think of my work in reproductive justice as the predominant positive I had been able to wring out of that history. All the hardship had led me to a certain purpose as an activist. So, when someone else claimed credit for a concept that was at the core of the transformative work my sisters and I had done, it felt like that legacy was rendered invisible like it might mean nothing after all.

That's why I was blinded by anger. I was hurting without knowing why, without knowing where I could put that pain. And, of course, I now know, I was not alone.

Hurt Can Hide Us or Unite Us

When we start with the self, our first step is to identify the impulses that prevent us from being present to help others. For me, the chief offender tends to be my unprocessed anger and more than a touch of ego. Others might be held back by a lack of confidence or a fear of making mistakes. (Psychologist Thomas Curran observes that most perfectionists have a lingering sense that they're the ones who are never quite perfect enough.) Others still might be falling short due to overconfidence or difficulty in truly listening to others.

Once we've identified those tendencies within ourselves, step two of starting with the self requires developing a tool kit of techniques that allow us to navigate around our roadblocks. We want to be able to put our weaknesses on pause for a spell so that we have the wherewithal to call others in with patience and care. We can even learn to recast our supposed "weaknesses" as strengths.

For example, I have to constantly remind myself to slow down, even if I think I know the answer. I must rein in my impatience with slower, more careful thinkers who frequently have more thoughtful contributions than people like me who blurt out the first thing that pops into our heads. Learning to appreciate that people have different ways of processing information helps me connect with many people I may have overlooked in the past.

It's all easy to say, of course, but more difficult to practice. Once I'd learned that my anger is rooted in pain, I had to become uncomfortably familiar with that pain as I've learned to call myself in. It was horrifying at first, but I've strangely found it easiest to face my pain by discussing it with others. Calling in works for me because I am willing to forego the relative safety of wounded silence. I first realized this when I spoke with William Fuller and Prisoners Against Rape.

One of the benefits of calling in is that it goes both ways. It can help all parties open up and heal their wounds through self-forgiveness. Once I started to talk more about my trauma, I was surprised at how often I found a certain recognition in others. Even if it manifests differently— not as anger but as fear, not as aggression but as avoidance—I saw how often each of our weaknesses is tied to some past point of pain. We all tend to see the world through the pain we've experienced. This is true of me, and it's true of many of us in activist circles, where it's common for people who've experienced trauma to orient our lives around alleviating the trauma of others. It's this fact that continues guiding me on my journey as a survivor and activist. I am slowly and painstakingly learning how to embrace calling in practices both to treat my wounds and to build our movement.

Pain and trauma aren't as simple to navigate, however. You can't will a wound to heal. Instead, I've slowly learned that something else is possible: when we call ourselves in, it's possible to shift our relationship to pain. When I sought to hide my pain and ignore it, my pain ended up controlling me. It made me isolated, small, fearful, vengeful.

Throughout my life, many of my call outs and power grabs—from my high school drill team to my mass email to Angela—sprang from feeling slighted. Trauma can make us unable to tell truth from tragedy. Even something minor can make me feel helpless in a way that arouses familiar emotions from my past assaults, feelings that most rape survivors cope with. I intellectually understand that the memories now welling up are not a sexual assault—but I'm being triggered all the same. It's only when I have the wherewithal to pause and start with myself that I can recognize that these triggers are just that: a restimulation of an event from my past, not an accurate response to what's happening in the present. So, while trusting my feelings is important, I've also had to learn that it's vital for me to understand *why* I have them so that I can make more accurate threat assessments and respond appropriately. If I let my pain, my anger, and my discomfort rule me, then I'll mistake ordinary situations for cruelty and abuse—because that's where my memories go.

Now, when I feel that familiar surge of anger, I start by taking note of what I'm feeling and labeling it as "anger." This is a popular technique in cognitive behavioral therapy—staying mindful of your emotional states so that you can recognize the symptoms right before you're swept up in a flood of emotion. It's like the "color wheel" for emotions, helping people identify what exactly they're feeling. If I catch my anger and realize that I don't have a productive reason for it, I can refuse to act on it. Instead, I call myself in with somatic activities to relax my body, like measured breathing or counting in my head.

In *Eloquent Rage: A Black Feminist Discovers Her Superpower*, Professor Brittney Cooper wrote: "My feelings, for their part, go on strike against me all the time, showing up with picket signs that scream truths I'd rather not hear." These activities can help slow me down and regain myself, whether I'm sitting at my computer or in a tense meeting. I put myself on pause, even as my heart is beating fast. Even as I feel like I'm in danger, I practice slowing myself down to deescalate. If I feel I need a time-out to become calm enough to have a productive conversation, I take it. An easy sentence to remember in situations like these is "Tell me more." This buys time, allowing me to fight the impulse to fight or shut down.

I sometimes rely on my sistafriends to safely discharge my anger when it threatens to shut down my brain. Picking up the phone to ask for shared time to vent is one of the calling in strategies I learned from workshops with Lillie Allen at the National Black Women's Health Project (now called the Black Women's Health Imperative). It's called "shared time" because I don't ask my friends for emotional labor without offering the same in return. And when I'm reenergized by the love of my friends, I can face life's challenges with hope and joy.

As adrienne maree brown said, "What we give attention to grows." What I focus on tends to be what consumes my attention at the expense of other options. So, I try to avoid feeding my frustration any more sustenance—it's living large without my help. And I've made anger-management techniques into daily rituals for myself, whether I'm letting go of the rage that surges when I scroll from one post to the next, or the pang I feel when someone cuts me off on my commute home. I've learned to monitor my protective mechanisms: disassociation, not giving a f**k, avoidance, feeling damaged. Instead of protecting me, these patterns close me off.

We must try to stay alert to how our pain can isolate us.

It takes a lifetime to understand and navigate our weaknesses. Yet that's the beauty of calling in: once you make room for forgiveness, the process doesn't need to be perfect. We can forgive ourselves for our weaknesses and still try to outsmart them—and over time this becomes a skill we can share. We can extend that forgiveness and grace to others when we call them in.

Transmuting Pain to Empathy

In my online courses, I often ask the participants how mistakes were handled when they were kids. If a child is severely punished and humiliated for making a mistake, then they grow up believing it is natural to shame and punish others—and themselves. They don't learn self-forgiveness. But if a child is forgiven for making a mistake and assured of love while they are taught its lesson, then as adults they are predisposed to forgive others and offer grace and respect. The choice for us as adults is whether we want to continue these harmful patterns of our childhood or make a different choice, whether the mistake is our own or someone else's.

It was only when I forgave myself for the pain I'd suffered, and the pain I'd passed along, that I recognized how pain was all around me—a common condition in so many of the people I encountered. And a point of connection: I understand something about them and they understand something about me. Even if someone else's pain looks different from mine, even if it doesn't amount to "as much" as what I've experienced, even if I could argue that I'd been tougher, stronger, braver—it doesn't matter. That competitive dynamic only breeds resentment. And the truth is that everyone's pain *hurts*. There are very few people who aren't navigating some form of pain or hardship or loss. Everyone deserves to have that weight eased.

Once I looked at my pain with forgiveness, I realized that I could use my pain to understand how others' actions might also be rooted in pain. I could even develop a kind of muscle memory for compassion. Calling in is not a one-and-done event. Learning these practices is an active engagement with the self in service to others. It's a dynamic process of inquiry, exploration, and growth.

With every conflict, we create a narrative. Social media has trained us to seek out and respond to the most striking and strident ones. But most scenarios aren't dripping with drama and gossip; most conflicts are born out of some combination of miscommunication, ignorance, and error. If none of those fit the bill, I can speak from experience in saying that pain and insecurity make up plenty of the difference. Even when someone's actions look like outright malice, there's quite often something more at play.

When we start with ourselves, part of our mission is to figure out whether we're ready to see the good in someone else, not just the bad. If we change what we look for, then the whole picture of a conflict can transform. We can look for a reason to understand someone rather than a reason to condemn them. And, from there, a call in becomes possible.

The counterpart to this sort of emotional intelligence is integrity intelligence. This means being aware of your values and living by them, committing to doing the right thing without rewards or witnesses. You can make difficult choices instead of easy excuses, prioritizing your integrity over your reputation so that no one can persuade you to do something against your honor and intelligence.

Don't Pressure Yourself

Calling in is radical imagination work that offers true revolutionary potential for changing our relationships with ourselves and the world.

There's a power, a muscularity to calling in. It requires emotional intelligence, the courage to overcome your fears, and an investment in another's growth without proof of return. The goal is not to assume the magical power to fix other people. It's to try to become your best self by offering love, respect, and compassion to those with whom you disagree. As difficult as it is, we can learn how to offer compassion for people who violate human rights. It's entirely too easy to look down on them, to think "I know the truth, and they don't," and to use our certitude to disregard their humanity. Calling in can allow us to heal—showing us how strong we can become—even as we offer others an outlet for their healing. It can allow us to be vulnerable and confident at the same time. But that's only if we are in the right place.

Realistically, we can't always respond with grace and understanding. As much as we may ask of ourselves, and as much work as we put into our healing, no one person is going to always be the right person to call *anyone* in, in *any* situation. Now may be a time to set boundaries and enforce them. If you are still actively hurting from your emotional wounds, your attempt to call another person in will likely end up damaging others because your pain will seep out. If your anger is pent up, you'll likely explode on the very person you're trying to help. If you have a particularly fraught relationship with someone who needs to be called in, it might be best to let a friend take the lead. It all depends on your self-assessment of your emotional state. But know this: no one is obligated to call another person in.

In 2016, my son, Howard, died at age forty-seven of a sudden heart attack. He had grown into an incredible man—a loving son and husband, an engineer and a professor, an organizer and a hobbyist—who left the world far too soon. After Howard's funeral, I received a voicemail from his paternal aunt, the sister of the man who abused me. I wasn't surprised she knew how to reach me; any relative could have easily provided my phone number. That's the strange intimacy of incest—the continuation of your vulnerability, even close to five decades on.

I was too angry to return her call. Why had it taken forty-seven years for her to contact me? Where was she when I was a teenager, struggling while parenting her nephew? Where was she when Howard was alive?

A few weeks later, I thought more about why she was calling, and why now. It suddenly dawned on me that she might have been offering—and seeking—compassion. I had learned through the family that her brother was a serial pedophile who had abused at least three different teenagers. I'd reckoned with my portion of that trauma, but how did this affect the rest of his family? And I had another horrible thought: Did he first start with her?

This offered a new way to understand her call—one that didn't lead me straight to negativity. I considered picking up the phone for quite some time and thought about the different ways the conversation could go. But I eventually decided not to. I wasn't ready to talk to her after all these years. If she was seeking to apologize, to offer her condolences, or share what she felt about her brother, I didn't think any of those things would make me feel any better. And if she was seeking compassion or sympathy, I wasn't the person who could offer it. I had to prioritize my healing, not stick a dagger back into wounds that were still barely closing.

I made an intentional choice not to call her in, as an act of self-preservation. Instead, I called it off. I was finished with letting my abuser make me feel re-raped again. Forty-seven years was enough.

We are all suffering from trauma to one degree or another. It might be multigenerational and inherited; it might be enmeshed in our place in society; it might take one of a myriad of deeply personal forms. But even if we suffer in unique ways, we all get to choose whether we make the situation worse or better by our response to it.

In more than five decades of working in activism, I've found that calling in is often the best response we can choose. It's not always perfect, and it's not always something we're up for. But that's just fine.

For a long time, I had no capacity for self-forgiveness: I would make mistakes and berate myself, which only created more self-loathing. But once I started to call myself in, I learned that I could be a publicly imperfect person working for a perfect cause. My potential was only limited by the amount of energy I was expending to keep my pain sealed inside and my mistakes hidden for fear of being called out.

I now try not to regret things that happened to me for fear of devaluing my hard-earned strengths and wisdom. This is something I've had to learn, and I learned it by starting with myself. Over time, it has become a kind of grace that I feel comfortable offering to others too, by calling them in when I see them struggling or suffering. It's this skill that I want to spread to readers of this book—and to the whole world of people who want to give up their rage for a chance at hope and healing.

So how do we do this? How do we call others in?

6.

CALLING IN TECHNIQUES

In recognizing the humanity of our fellow beings,
we pay ourselves the highest tribute.

—Thurgood Marshall

I have run hundreds of classes and workshops in my career. I've spoken to FBI agents about federal hate crimes. I've keynoted conferences on the latest needs of the reproductive justice movement. I've led seminars on college greens and met with white supremacists on Appalachian mountain tops. I've wrangled with business leaders and academics, neocons, and leftists alike.

And I've learned that there is one constant: At nearly every event, there is a Ron (or Rhonda).

Ron is the person who will raise his hand at the first call for questions or race up to the Q&A mic. He is in the audience, but you get the feeling he would rather be onstage. Ron has decided, either consciously or unconsciously, to see if the workshop should be about him. Ron is often male but not always, often white but not always. He may as well be there to test you. To tempt you.

One night, Ron may have prepared a monologue with no question in sight about a recent conversation he had with a second cousin about the American toad, which he thinks the whole audience will find interesting. Another evening, Ron leads with a joke about woke culture, but don't get mad, it's just a joke. And he does have a question: What about him? He grew up poor and white; does he really have white privilege? On a different day, Ron might chime in to inform an auditorium full of people that we don't say "auditorium" anymore because it is ableist. Ron has determined it's problematic. He's made a habit of manufacturing offense.

Ron is the person you want to call out, badly. He is minor conflict and distraction embodied. He is "just asking questions," countering every point with "what about so-and-so," invoking the "Oppression Olympics," and playing it all off as "just a joke." Ron exists in person and online; he can find you at the workplace watercooler, plop down across from you at Thanksgiving dinner, or materialize in your DMs. Sometimes, he is a troll, goading you to snap at him. More often, he's some combination of confused and overconfident, insecure and misinformed, genuinely curious and well-meaning. As neuropsychology professor Robert Hanlon said, "Never attribute to malice that which is adequately explained by stupidity." But one thing's for sure: Ron's comments are well off the mark.

Every time he appears, Ron presents you with a choice. Ron is the lightning rod we could vent our frustration upon if we let ourselves lose sight of our larger goals.

Sure, you could challenge Ron's denial of his white privilege, explaining that, to borrow writer Walter Rhein's helpful comparison, "You might not have robbed the bank, but you were the one who spent the money." But this could be a disruption.

So, are you going to call out Ron—for derailing the conversation, for regurgitating flawed talking points, for being clueless enough to drone on and on?

Or are you going to call him in?

And if you're going to call him in, what does that look like?

Learning why we call in is one thing, but learning how is another. A large part of the challenge lies in the baggage and assumptions that each of us brings to any conflict. That's why we start with the self. But we're also approaching others who have their assumptions and baggage, and who may not always be in the best place themselves. Even if we're personally feeling ready, calling in is still a skill and an art. It takes both practice and improvisation.

Each call in will be different, just as each conflict and conversation we encounter is unique. But, over the years, I've distilled an effective strategy for calling in. I'll present it here in a few discrete steps, which you can follow from the first flare-up:

1.   Start with the self.
2.   Calibrate the conflict.
3.   Approach with love.
4.   Accept the reaction.
5.   Reach a resolution.

1) Start with the Self

I've already covered the importance of starting with the self, which is a long-term effort. It takes time to bring ourselves to a place where anger, pain, and trauma aren't steering our day-to-day emotions. But there is also heat-of-the-moment work.

Let's say I'm running a workshop and someone sidles up to the Q&A mic. "You seem nice and all," Ron says, "but how is all this 'woke' talk actually relevant to me?"

Or perhaps I'm a young feminist activist seeking to discuss sterilization abuse with my boss, and she responds, "Sterilization abuse?" as if the phrase is an oxymoron.

Or I might be running an anti-hate meeting in rural Appalachia when one of the Klan wives I'm working with calls me "the colored girl."

What do you do the split second after someone has let their tongue run wild?

The first thing to do is to put yourself on pause. Your heart may be beating fast, and you may experience a feeling of danger. But if we've been working on ourselves, we can recognize what's happening. And we can recognize that there is a choice standing in between our emotions and our actions.

So, I'll try to breathe deeply. I'll nod along for a moment until I've made my choice. Sometimes, I'll need an extra beat to steady myself. So, I'll pass the ball back to the other person's court by saying something neutral: "Could you say more?" I might ask. "I'm not sure I understand what you mean."

Meanwhile, I will check in with myself to decide whether I'm ready to call someone in. The question I ask myself is this: What is in my heart right now? When I peer inside, do I see only anger, frustration, stress, and exhaustion? Or can I also find empathy, curiosity, patience, or love? If the answer is "all negative," then I know I'm not ready to call anyone in. Nor should I be calling anyone out. If negative energy is the only fuel available, we're liable to make things worse, even when a call out is justified.

If I can't find positive emotions, I'll seek to end the conversation or deflect it to another time—even if I'm not doing so gracefully. "That's a good question," I might tell Ron when he asks about "woke" language. "We're all trying to learn which ideas work best for us today. If any takeaways stick with you, why don't you let me know what landed after the session? Now, does anyone else have other questions?" Just keep it short and neutral—even if it's through gritted teeth.

On the other hand, when I do feel that reserve of positive emotions within, that's when I'll be able to go deeper. I will move on to step two of a call in: trying to understand the root conflict and the person I'm trying to reach.

2) Calibrate the Conflict

Conflict is like an iceberg: There's the obvious disagreement. But there are also—inevitably—complicated dynamics lurking below the surface. Any time we're working with interpersonal issues—where communication styles, personalities, backgrounds, or politics don't fully align—much of the conflict will dwell below what's being said.

When Ron gets up at the mic and asks what all this "woke talk" means for him, my first thought isn't a thought; it's pure reaction. A tightness, a wariness, a weariness. Because Ron is using "woke" in a way that I don't expect to hear in that room. He's using it as my 0 percent opponents tend to use it, with ridicule, dismissiveness, or even hostility. So, I clock him as a potential threat, and many of my closest allies in the audience have the same reaction. I can feel a ripple of tension spread throughout the room.

But I take a moment as Ron finishes talking. I calm the immediate threat response that's blaring in my head like a siren. I search for the reserve of curiosity within that will allow me to consider a call in. Then I calibrate.

How serious does the conflict appear at first glance? Is the person I'm confronting trying to be threatening and confrontational?

If someone is shouting insults and rushing toward me, I'm not going to stick around to find out what else is going on in their life. I'm checking out of there! When imminent harm is on the table, that's when our fight-or-flight mode is warranted.

But if the situation is calmer—if everyone is keeping their hands to themselves, even if voices are raised—then we can assess harm and intent more deliberately. I'll ask myself three questions to gauge what's going on: (1) Have I or someone else been wronged in this situation? (2) Have I been wronged intentionally? (3) And am I certain that it was intentional and not a result of ignorance, stupidity, or miscommunication?

If I answer yes to all three questions, then I'm in a situation where a call out is warranted. But if my answer to any of them is no, then I will steer toward a call in, especially if I think there's more than malice in play. That means there's likely to be more below the surface, which might offer a path to understanding.

Admittedly, it can be difficult to assess the distinction between intentional malice and honest ignorance. And I don't want to allow people to evade accountability or to accept facile excuses for abusive behaviors. Often, people will pretend to be unaware of the impact of their words or actions. And we should not minimize the significance of oppressive behavior, even if it's made with good intentions. Anyone can admit they've made a mistake and take responsibility for the harm they've caused.

In the case of Ron's question, an initial threat assessment leads me toward a call in. Ron's question gave me a jolt at first, but when I began to calibrate the conflict, I realized that I had no great reason—other than my own irritation—to call him out. He may be saying "woke" in the same tone as a Fox News talking head, but that's not posing a real threat to me or the audience. He's causing more annoyance and disruption than harm. He might just enjoy being a jerk. Or he might not even realize that he's disrupting the event, and that possibility sparks my curiosity.

What lies below the surface of the conflict?

On the surface, Ron is asking a simple question: "How do I use the material you're discussing?" But just a layer below, his language is charged. "Woke talk" makes it sound like he's being dismissive or provocative, acting like a troll who wants to spark a backlash. He might be deliberately trying to disrupt the event, recenter the conversation on his priorities, and get a call out clip for his YouTube channel. So I want to keep my cool in case he wants an emotional reaction from me.

Folks who maliciously try to get attention by taking words out of context or presenting "evidence" that doesn't make sense should be quickly dismissed. I'll say something like, "We're sticking to the topic of the discussion right now. Perhaps you can come back when you've caught up. Next!" What I don't do is try to correct them, argue with them, or let them dominate the conversation with their non sequiturs.

But when I calibrated the conflict, I decided there was a good chance Ron was completely unaware of the trip wire of a word he'd chosen. If he's someone who's a 50 percent ally or further out, he might not know the nuances or contexts of language that's second nature to my closer allies. This might mean he's genuinely trying to learn, and he's brave enough to do so while standing at a microphone in front of strangers. In that case, I certainly don't want to ruin his day.

There's also a third possibility, where Ron is somewhere in the middle, stuck in his own internal conflict. This is something I see often in workshop settings. Participants enter hoping to learn about activism and inequality, but they also find themselves challenged in uncomfortable ways. That pull between growth and insecurity creates a tug-of-war that is difficult to self-manage. Ron might be used to being in control, and today he has absorbed a bunch of ideas about privilege and patriarchy that have disrupted his sense of self. So, by asking a question or delivering a lengthy "more of a comment than a question," Ron can eke some measure of control out of an environment where he's not the boss. And if he asks a question that puts the onus on me, then he can even use it to solve his own internal conflict.

For instance, if I don't give Ron a convincing answer about what wokeness can do for him, then he can have an excuse to reaffirm his skepticism. If I grow annoyed or call him out, then he can rest assured I don't live up to the higher values I claim to try to live by, so why listen to anything else? Either outcome would resolve the deeper conflict that's driving Ron's question—the insecurity that's roiling within—even if Ron doesn't realize what he's doing.

People are complicated. We're moved by impulses that often contradict. And one of the most powerful drives is that we are always searching for control, often because of untreated anxiety or trauma from our childhood. We also frequently assume ill intent about things that bother us while forgetting that we are not the center of everyone else's attention.

Calling in allows us to get used to seeking the depths that can lurk under even simple conflicts. I don't need to spend an hour trying to psychoanalyze Ron; I don't want to make too many assumptions. Instead, a quick "maybe he's an asshole, or maybe it's something else" will suffice. From there, perhaps I can move beyond the surface-level conflict—trying to define "woke" for Ron—if I realize throughout the conversation that what he really wants is something else: to feel welcomed and reassured that it's not too late or too hard for him, too, to do good.

Of course, no one is going to fault me if I don't try to look at the different layers of the conflict. There's a world in which Ron just looks like a jerk to me, and I respond in a way that makes him think I'm a jerk too. We cross paths, then recoil, winding up further apart and with our guards up.

But if I accept that conflict can run deeper, I can try to give him a bit of grace before I pass judgment. Doing so is not always easy, and not always possible, but I want it to be my goal—because there is also a world where a bit of understanding and patience allows two distant figures to enter the same movement rather than opposing ones.

Who am I addressing? What are the power dynamics in play?

Just as we consider the depths of the conflict, we need to consider the person we're calling in. Are you calling in a stranger, or do you have a preexisting relationship that will affect whether they might be receptive to your gesture? Are you calling in someone who has less power and privilege than you, or someone who has more, or someone with roughly the same? These power dynamics are critical, because they affect your counterpart's ability to hear what you're saying, and their ability to respond honestly.

With Ron, if I'm onstage and have an audience attentive to my every word, then I'm in a clear position of power compared to him. Even if I'm worried that he's a provocateur, he's not on his home turf. So, it would be very easy for me to turn that room against him and draw out the anger of the mob. I also have the leeway to interrupt if

I want. This means I can and should be slower to reach for a call out. I need to use my power wisely.

How will your call in unfold? What might happen in the best-case scenario? What about the worst-case scenario? Can you address the conflict right now? Or is it likely to spiral into a distraction . . . or worse?

I want to be intentional about the setting of a call in. So I try to envision how the conversation will be received by the recipient and anyone else who's in the room. If I think I can address Ron's concerns in a way that will help him and the audience learn something together, then I'll take the time to call him in right there. But if I can only imagine it distracting from the conversation at hand, or if time is getting short and others want to speak, then I'll deflect. I will also deflect if I realize I might just be gearing up to embarrass Ron in front of the crowd, which is a gift I reserve for only the worst trolls.

As I run through the possible scenarios, it's impossible to imagine every way a call in could unfold. I'm not trying to plan for every contingency. I'm just trying to figure out if the worst-case scenario might outweigh the best-case scenario. If I see red flags adding up, I may choose another of the 5Cs and call it off.

That's what I did when one of the women in the Tennessee quilting group that was a front for KKK wives referred to me as "the colored girl" and I decided not to even mention it. Why? Because we were working on more important goals. We had just managed to convene for a vulnerable conversation where the women could speak openly about the hate, violence, and fear in their lives. If I policed their language at the first opportunity, the space for open conversation would have closed. And I could tell that the woman who said "colored girl" was trying to be polite; she just didn't know the right language. The harm was minor, and negative intent was absent. The opportunity for growth was greater if I kept the meeting on track. I saw that even the best-case scenario call in would have accomplished little. So I let it go.

3) Lead with Love

Let's say you're ready for the conversation. You're facing down Ron, and you're determined not to call him out, even though he's riled you up. You've tried to understand where he's coming from and where the call in might go. Now, what do you say first?

When you go to look Ron in the eye and initiate your call in, the three words to remember are these: "lead with love."

I prefer to start with simple questions to get a conversation rolling without precipitating guilt and shame. I'm a fan of conversation prompts. So here are some of the lines that I've found helpful:

- "When you said _____, I didn't understand what you meant. Do you have time for us to talk about it more?"
- "Can I revisit something you said? It felt harsh to me, and I'm sure you didn't mean it that way."
- "When you used that word, I heard it differently. Can we talk about what it means?"
- "I beg your pardon. I don't understand what you mean, and I'd like to."
- "I know you, and I know you're a kind person. But this phrase felt off when I heard you say it."
- "I was surprised when you said _____. Is everything all right? Is there something else on your mind?"

At first glance, each of these prompts might seem a little placating. You might be thinking that we're letting the other person off the hook. Maybe you're thinking: "I know exactly what they meant when they 'misspoke,' and they're lucky I'm deciding to be nice today!" When I first began trying to call people in, that's all I could think about. I couldn't get my mind away from the fact that I was holding back and that I was doing them a favor by letting them start on my good side. Inevitably, I just ended up calling them out five minutes later instead of immediately.

That's call out culture for you: the idea that withholding judgment for a few minutes is a favor. That's why I now try to treat "love" as the ideal.

The idea, when starting a call in, is to invite your counterpart to think about what they're saying, thinking, and presenting to the world. You want to let them know that their words are landing astray, and you want to prompt them to reassess what they're saying. At the same time, you want to reassure them that you really are open to mutual growth, even if that growth involves making more mistakes.

How you phrase the invitation for further communication makes an enormous difference. The provided open-ended prompts encourage people to share not only their thoughts but also the feelings underlying their thinking. They also suggest that no matter how controversial the person's opinions are, this is a welcome time to share them.

Sometimes a basic calling in prompt is all it takes for a Ron to realize that he's made a mistake. More often, your initial prompt is the start of a longer conversation or even a series of conversations. If you're in public, these prompts invite the audience to weigh in on the discussion as well, alleviating the fear that they will be publicly shamed if they have questions that reveal their own learning curves.

You are rarely going to convince a person all at once that they're wrong, or that they need to change. And, paradoxically, the harder you try to change someone, the more they're going to resist. That's the strategic error that call outs make: they push people to repent immediately, which sends them into a fight-or-flight mode.

There's a similar strategic error that call ins can fall into, however, if you're not careful. If you start a call in trying too hard to change someone else, most people can sniff that out a mile away. And no one wants to be lectured at—even in a patient tone. We can only consider changing and growing if we're approached as equals.

It's important, then, to see calling in conversations as exchanges of perspectives. If a call in is going to be effective, we shouldn't be heading in dead-set that we're 100 percent correct and they're 100 percent wrong. We shouldn't anticipate that we'll do all the teaching and they'll do all the learning. Part of why I like open-ended prompts is that they invite us to learn something about what's driving others, and often to trade stories of our own experiences.

For example, this might be an opportunity to share with Ron and the audience my own journey to "wokeness." Being raised by conservative parents did not prepare me for the dramatic social changes of the 1960s. When my friends in the Black nationalist movement insisted that I learn to use their preferred Africanized names instead of what they called their "slave" names, it was disconcerting. I'm still learning new things every day, like stumbling over pronouns. My intentions may be commendable, but my habits can still be problematic.

Remembering how embarrassed I felt when I forgot someone's new name or pronoun may help me empathize with Ron's feeling of being left behind. So I assure him that he's welcome in the calling in movement, even if he disagrees with all this "woke" talk. It's not about who is the most "woke" but who is willing to be kind and inviting to others. Is this something he'd like to try?

We can learn how to use calling in techniques through repetition, developing small habits, and practicing the way we learn any new skill. For now, start with a couple of prompts that make sense to you. From there, be patient with yourself and with others, and you'll start to see it become easier and easier to achieve empathy, curiosity, and even love.

4) Accept the Reaction

It can feel abysmal to be on the wrong end of a call out. But being called in doesn't always feel much better.

When we seek to call someone in, we know that we're trying to be kind and understanding. But that's not always obvious on the other end. It's perfectly natural for anyone who's being called in to experience the same fight-or-flight panic that they would with a call out. They're being challenged, and they don't know whether you're going to go scorched earth or offer a fig leaf. In that moment of confusion, they might argue back against you. They might shut down and remain silent. They might seek to leave or end the conversation. They might be panicked, ashamed, or distraught.

Any of these reactions might rebound back at you. You can do as much work as you'd like in advance—trying to plan out the conversation and imagine how it will go—but it will never go completely as planned. Never. And the trick to ensuring a successful call in is to accept the unexpected reaction that rushes back at you.

Say I'd decided to adjust one of my standard prompts to call Ron in. He had asked what "woke talk" could do for him, and I'd realized it was hard to see where the conversation would go without first knowing what the phrase meant to him.

"That's a good question, Ron," I say. "We're all here trying to learn how we can treat one another more kindly and how we can grow together without fighting so much along the way. But let me make sure I understand what that's bringing up for you right now. What do you mean when you say 'woke talk'? And what are you hoping you'll learn from being here today?"

"I don't know," Ron says. "I mean, all the concern around everyone's feelings. It's just . . . it makes me so annoyed."

Or he might say: "It makes me feel left, out if I'm honest," and we have a different conversation.

Or he says: "I want to help but don't know how."

Or he says: "I want to try to explain it to my son, but he's just furious all the time."

There are a lot of different conversations to be had, and if you're trying chiefly to steer people to your line of thinking, then it can be overwhelming to prepare for them all. Instead, we want to be ready to accept a range of reactions.

True change is hard, and it takes time—longer than any single conversation. It's unlikely that we're going to win over all our 50 percent allies or our 75 percent allies, even if we bring up talking points and data. So we should stand up for our values—without anger or reproach. But it isn't realistic to expect to win even a handful of converts through brilliant debating. A conversation gets a lot easier—for all parties—if it's running on an obvious agenda of empathy and respect.

And remember, we don't need full agreement on everything. I like to say that our larger goal when calling in is to persuade people to *be* with us, not to *agree* with us. Think back to chapter 3: it's perfectly fine for our 90 percent and 75 percent allies to disagree with us on some points. As long as we can stand together for the largest issues, we're in good shape. Plus, we create a more welcoming atmosphere if we're not needling people over every disagreement. We can allow people to consider us and our ideas in their own time.

We don't always need to be preparing our next argument. As my elders counseled me, if you don't have something positive to say, try shutting up. I wished I'd listened to this wise advice earlier—but that was my problem: I didn't know how to listen. Calling in works best when we embrace listening. An engaged, active listener seeks to absorb another person's idea and then offer them back in our own words, to make sure we understand. An engaged, active listener is also attuned to context, body language, and silences, which contain stores of meaning when conflict is in the air. This helps us to figure out what's behind the person's words.

When we lead with listening, we're able to accept the person's reaction and adapt to whatever unexpected route a call in takes. If Ron pushes back and argues, I can postpone the discussion by suggesting that we talk one-on-one after the event. This indicates that I take his concerns seriously, but that I will not derail the event for the rest of the audience, depriving other participants of an opportunity to ask questions. I usually say that part out loud so that everyone in the room understands and can participate in keeping the event on track. (Of course, if Ron at this point becomes more committed to making a scene than to having his concerns addressed, then I treat him like a troll and point this out to the audience so that they understand why I'm handling the situation in this specific way.)

If, however, Ron reacts with tears or grief, then it's time to slow down. Often, I'll ask an audience member to please get up and stand in solidarity with him (without touching him). It's important to demonstrate to a person in pain that they are not alone, even symbolically. If Ron needs more time to process his emotions, I'll sometimes ask for a volunteer from the audience to assist him by providing a listening ear off to the side. This is a familiar tactic from the anti-rape movement—letting a person have their feelings in a safe enough space that doesn't interfere with other necessary conversations. I'll then check back on the pair of them after the event to see if they need additional support.

If Ron reacts to my attempt to call him in with silence or by disengaging, I need to appreciate that he is not ready to engage vocally, which is his right. No one should be forced to speak up or be judged simply because they don't have the words for how they feel in the moment.

It's also important to remember that silence does not equal consent. When I was with SisterSong, I had to learn that when some of our members were silent, that was a sign we needed to slow down. The silence was not always resistance so much as a signal that the time had not yet come for this conversation. So we slept on it and came back another time.

If, however, Ron agrees with what I say as I begin to call him in and seems willing to listen, I can use this as an opportunity for further engagement. Perhaps I might connect with him after the event or provide information on how to get involved in his local community.

5) Reach a Resolution

How do we want to close our calling in conversations? How do we square empathy with accountability?

Calling in takes an approach that might seem less results-oriented than calling out. But in many scenarios—especially when we're calling out allies or potential allies over small mistakes or narrow differences—we've seen how calling out can backfire, causing enmity and division rather than actual reform. Calling in moves slower, but more reliably. It aims to help people understand how they're causing harm, why that's an issue, and how they can improve.

Underlying calling in are the notions of restorative justice and transformative justice. Scholar and activist Fania E. Davis describes restorative justice as "a justice that is not about getting even but getting well." It seeks to find forgiveness, if forgiveness is possible, by bringing victim and perpetrator together—often in the presence of a facilitator—so the violator can take responsibility for their actions, express remorse, and make amends. This is psychologically important for the person who experienced harm because, as Davis observes, an unhealthy emphasis on revenge "locks us into the past and tethers us to . . . an overidentification with the pain, mistaking it for who we really are. This attachment to suffering blocks the path to healing, magnifies vengeance, and expands pain."

One difference between restorative justice and transformative justice is that restorative justice seeks to make the person who has experienced harm whole again while transformative justice goes deeper, examining root causes and seeking to address the context under which the harm occurred. For example, when a person is robbed, a restorative justice process might see the robber take responsibility for their actions, apologize, and return what was stolen, while transformative justice interrogates the conditions that caused the robbery to occur. Was the perpetrator hungry? Did they have another unmet need? How can the community collectively address both the conditions that cause harm to occur and the socialized trauma—like feeling unsafe—that everyone in the community experiences as a result? Transformative justice deindividualizes responsibility, suggesting that the entire community shares the responsibility for preventing harm, and helping those who are harmed be "restored" without causing more harm to the community.

This is the type of resolution we hope to attain through calling in. But when we're in the middle of a calling in conversation, it can be difficult for a beginner to see how to steer the conversation in the direction of accountability, restoration, or transformation.

The first step is to make sure that we're communicating to the other person that their behavior—even if it has a perfectly reasonable explanation—wasn't innocuous. In one of my online trainings, for example, a blind participant spoke about how she hated random strangers placing their hands on her when she needed to open a door or walk up steps. Because she couldn't see the uninvited touch coming, it felt like an assault and so she'd lash out.

Many instances of harm are simply a matter of this sort of "bad kindness" or poorly thought-out efforts at being kind. To steer someone who's done this toward accountability and transformation, you might try these three steps:

1. Thank the person for their good intentions. While innocuous intent does not excuse harm, people are more likely to take ownership of the impact of their actions if consideration is given to their intent.

2. Let them know what they aren't doing right. In this case, the participant could let them know she doesn't like strangers touching her and she's setting her boundary.

3. Guide them to what would work instead. Perhaps asking first?

Depending on the situation, it may also help to share mistakes we've made along the way, so the person we're calling in feels less singled out.

If the harm is bad enough, we should also encourage people to seek to restore what damage they can by making amends to the victims. (I'll explain how to make amends in chapter 8.) One of the underlying assumptions of a call out is that the damage has been done and nothing can fix it—which is why we sometimes seek to punish or cancel the perpetrator. But that's zero-sum, prison-industrial thinking. When we move to the restorative framework of calling in, we can move beyond that. Even though the first mistake doesn't go away, it becomes something we can make up for through future success.

So where does that leave Ron? Standing on that stage, I'm not looking for any dramatic gotcha moment. I don't need to lecture him in front of a whole audience just to get him to realize that he's using "woke" in a way that gives me the heebie-jeebies. Instead, I'd hope to have enough of a conversation in a few short moments to give him a sense that social justice terminology isn't just talk. And, more important, I'd reassure him that there's a spot for him within the human rights movement, anytime, if he wants it.

That's the resolution, after all, that addresses the root of the conflict: Ron's uncertainty about his own belonging. If I'm in a good place, I would even try to find a way to hold him accountable for getting more involved—whether that's as simple as inviting him out to another event or linking him up with local activist groups. But even after I extend an invitation to participate in building the human rights movement, Ron may not be ready. He may need to process this new information at his own pace. That's okay. Because there will be other opportunities for someone else to call Ron in, especially as we spread this culture shift more broadly.

And as we move further and further beyond our 90 percent spheres of influence, we'll never lack for new Rons who challenge us to live up to our values.

7.

CREATING A CALL IN CULTURE

I may be wrong and you may be right,
and by an effort, we may get nearer to the truth.

—Karl Popper

When I walked in the door, the scene was raucous: the space aglow in neon and blacklight, flashes of ruby and gold glistening off disco balls. Club music thrummed, as an emcee took up a mic and began working the crowd.

I was at a drag queen lip sync fundraiser to support SisterLove, a Black women's HIV/AIDS organization founded by my best friend, Dázon Dixon Diallo. I'd never been to a drag show before, and it seemed like a perfect opportunity to indulge my curiosity while backing a worthy cause.

Once the room was in a crescendo, the queens made their entrance, wild costumes—feathers, lace, leather, fishnets—complemented by even wilder moves. Hips shook and backs curved. High heels hit the floor, then flipped skyward. The audience roared in excitement, throwing dollar bills onstage, and even tucking bills into their costumes as the performers strutted into the crowd.

I reached up to throw my handful of dollars as a performer approached. To my surprise, she smiled at me flirtatiously. Then she boldly grabbed my breast and squeezed, before shimmying back to the stage with a dramatic hair toss.

Only later, once all the dollar bills had been scooped up and the lights had come back on, did I have the chance to reflect on that moment and wonder why it hadn't even occurred to me to call her out. Going in, I certainly didn't expect to be fondled. And if the same thing had happened in *any* other environment, I realized, I would have been mortified. I would have been loud enough to drown out the bass and clear the room—plus the next one over. But in that fun atmosphere, I'd been comfortable enough to let my guard down and *keep it down*.

That's the thing, I realized: context matters. Why? Because I felt safe. When I'm in a setting that sets me on edge, I might have a hair trigger for any remark that puts my dignity in doubt. But I've worked for many years now on healing from my sexual assaults; I've learned to manage my involuntary triggers enough that, when I feel in control, I can let something that'd otherwise make me uneasy slide. I can experience something that isn't right without the reflexive urge to call a person out then and there.

Even as I'm telling this story, I'm wondering if I should. I don't want to provide ammunition to bigots who'll probably take it out of context to harm people I deeply care about. But I eventually decided to include it because, if not this story, they'll cherry-pick something else I've said to distort for their own nefarious purposes. I always remind myself that haters do what they do because of who they are, not what I do.

Now, I'm not going to be breaking out the fishnets. Not in this century. But I have become conscious over the years of how a call in culture is something we can *create*. I'm conscious of how grace, joy, and trust are all emotions that can flow effortlessly in the right setting. Once we understand the basic techniques of calling in, we can move on to the work of sharing them. From the workplace to the family room to the classroom, even to the wilds of the internet, we can create a new and necessary antidote to the call out culture: a *call in culture*. Our culture is defined by what we are for, not just what we are against. Where we reject the notion that we are only defined by our bad choices or silliest mistakes. Where we can move in the direction of our higher selves, not our deepest fears.

We know that calling in requires preparation. That's why we start with the self and calibrate the conflict before launching ourselves into the fray. But preparing ourselves only takes us so far. We don't want to work alone, siloed, and struggling in parallel; we want to be part of a movement, where we can support one another and accomplish our shared ends, together. This is why calling in is at its most powerful when it becomes a common culture within groups, schools, workplaces, and families. When we create a call in culture *before* tensions flare, we can fall back on shared values and procedures rather than letting our fear and anger send us straight into call out mode. We don't have to figure out an emergency plan only once the emergency has struck; we can start now and so weather conflicts that might otherwise tear us apart.

A Cry for Help: Creating a Call In Culture within Organizations

Most leaders in corporate C-suites once thought that their worst critics were their competitors. Now, they're discovering that they can be on their own payroll. Today's workforce is younger, queerer, more female, more intersectional, and less patient with inequities in the workplace than they used to be. They are concerned about respect, not just a paycheck. And they reasonably expect day-to-day practices to match the high moral language companies are using in public-facing communications. Proclaiming a commitment to gender equality and ending racial discrimination rings hollow when these pronouncements are not reflected in internal hiring, compensation, and promotion practices.

Many institutions are unprepared for this dramatic shift in priorities among employees. Bringing in new energy and perspectives can be energizing and enervating at the same time. Generational divides can make managing organizations more difficult, and in a call out atmosphere, normal workplace grievances can become wrapped up in broader racial and gender social inequities. Instead of using institutional channels to complain, employees are just as likely to use their keyboards to call out their employers on Slack or TikTok, making what was once viewed as private issues public. Most employers are not prepared to address personnel issues publicly—in fact, doing so may be prohibited by law— which means that only one side of the conflict becomes known.

Other employees self-censor for fear of being called out. They withhold their good ideas, terrified of social repercussions. Our call out culture reinforces people's timidity instead of making them braver in addressing unfair situations. We need a way of providing feedback that helps everyone not only feel included but also encouraged to contribute. Luckily, organizations—from the most storied institutions to the newest student groups—have one big thing going for them when it comes to creating a culture of calling in: an incentive to make things work. As political theorist Mie Inouye observed, "No conflict is productive without a social context that holds people together long enough that they have to try to understand where the other person is coming from. If we don't have to stay in the room together, we have no reason to do the difficult work of identifying the roots of our disagreement . . . and exercising our judgment to resolve the dispute."

When organizations ask me to help them create a call in culture, my approach is to concentrate on two concepts that any group can develop and implement: *advance understanding* and *advance accountability*. The first is a shared set of ideas, terms, and values that prepare us to understand potential conflicts; the second is a shared set of systems for navigating any conflicts that arise.

Advance Understanding

Advance understanding is just what it sounds like: a shared way of understanding conflict in advance of an actual flare-up. It means talking about calling in and calling out together as a group and getting on the same page. I like to hold meetings where the whole organization—or a series of breakout groups—can discuss their understanding of conflict and power dynamics. The goal is to draw everyone to a common language for navigating conflict—*not* to litigate any current grievances. A skilled facilitator can be very helpful.

You can start by helping people to recognize their own tendencies to engage in call out culture. Ask individuals to explain what conflict looks like to them, and how it has appeared in past workplaces or groups. You can ask them to list and define the specialized and nuanced terms that they commonly use when discussing conflict, words like sexism, racism, trigger, toxic, and microaggression.

Take time to discuss these terms and what they describe. Once everyone has had their say, your next goal is to come to a rough consensus on what these words mean within this particular group. For instance, you might define being "triggered" by its more serious and clinical use—being trapped in the memory of past trauma—not just feeling uncomfortable. There is no consensus on the meaning of these "spearpoint" words, as a feminist sociologist and trans Latina writer Katherine Cross terms them, so groups can collaboratively define what they'll mean in this specific setting. You might also draw from this book's previous chapters to define "constructive" and "destructive" call outs and to identify calling in as a loving, non-hostile alternative.

Note that there's a big debate around these fighting words, and at times a tendency to reach for euphemisms instead. For example, sometimes I'll say something is racist, while at other times I'll call someone "racially challenged." Generally, my choice depends on whether I think the person is trying to do better. I also try to read the room. If a group is less fragile and more open to frank discussions, I might say racist. But if tension is high and I want to offer some space for participants to consider if the word applies to them, I'll use a euphemism because the point is to keep them listening rather than defensively shutting down.

You'll want to find a common language for a range of different conflicts, wrongs, and disagreements that are likely to occur. And you'll then want participants to discuss what they consider appropriate responses to each. For instance, you could prompt participants to consider the difference between openly insulting behavior and a subtler microaggression, both in terms of intent and impact. We tend to judge people, not situations, as if context doesn't matter. So it's worth establishing that there are different ranges of offense and insult and different causes as well. Some conflicts do boil down to aggression and malice, but many that you'll encounter as a group are the result of someone muddling through an awkward conversation and misstepping along the way. It's important to differentiate between the two.

You can continue this conversation by asking people to discuss how they react when call outs occur. Do they respond with silence? Aggression? Gossiping behind others' backs? When we understand how others tend to respond when their first impulse gets its way, we can recognize when conflict starts to spread unnecessarily and do our best to steer it back toward a healthy call in. The point is not to encourage public confessions but for everyone to think about their patterns and to ask themselves is this the best they can do.

Our goal in identifying these different degrees and sources of conflict is to create a culture where we're not treating every offense as an emergency. Instead, we're creating channels for deescalating conflicts. And we're defining terms that allow us to discuss disagreements precisely before friction causes fire.

It is also important to discuss in advance of a conflict what to do with claims of unverifiable harm. If someone says they have been hurt, you certainly don't want to disbelieve them. But this doesn't automatically make the person being accused guilty. Thus, it becomes vital to establish ahead of need how such charges will be handled, providing support for both the accused and the accuser. The more open and impartial the process, the more likely both will feel they were treated fairly and compassionately. The same goes for anonymous claims of injury or harm, which frequently arise when there are fears of retaliation or a large power difference. Such reports should be taken seriously, but with the understanding that it would be irresponsible to blow up someone's career solely because of an anonymous charge.

Another option for building advance understanding is drama and role play. You can brainstorm as a group hypothetical examples of conflict—say, witnessing a microaggression, or realizing that you've said something out of line—and then ask people to practice how they would want to react in this scenario. This works best after reviewing the common language and going over basic calling in techniques so that participants can practice ready responses for steering potential call outs into call ins. Practice, within a controlled environment, helps people prepare for the real and unexpected situations that will inevitably arise. And it creates a culture where people feel confident that they can talk through tensions rather than bottling them up or explosively releasing them.

Advance Accountability

Advance understanding is about trying to reach a shared perspective on conflict before a crisis arises. *Advance accountability*, on the other hand, is about creating a set of practices that we can use to navigate conflicts once they've erupted. This enables us to offer a compassionate response to the predictable passion people experience in volatile situations. We don't need to feel like we're racing to defuse a ticking bomb—because we've already created our ground rules.

What should these ground rules look like? They need to give us a pathway through the conflict while considering both the person who's been wronged and the person who's caused the wrong. They need to make it easy for *anyone* to speak up—especially against groupthink—without fear of censure, whether they're speaking from a position of power or the margins. And, finally, they need to offer routes to real accountability, so that individuals can make amends for wrongs they've committed, whether intentionally or not.

Full accountability requires an honest assessment of the wrongs we do to each other. We're trying not to overinflate or minimize the harm, just to rigorously investigate how the injury occurred. Call outs often breed fear and dishonesty, as people try to evade punishment rather than telling the truth and owning their mistakes. So our goal is to provide a setting where it's *easier* to own the truth than to lie.

There are several approaches to achieving advance accountability. Every group is going to be different, so there's no one-size-fits-all prescription. Herewith, I've outlined several successful models that you can try out, choose from, and build on.

Create Call In Agreements

When you're calling in someone who isn't familiar with the difference between a call out and a call in, you're fighting an uphill battle. You'll need to calm their fight-or-flight response, while also keeping yourself calm. Calling in is much easier when you've already set some ground rules. You're still going to encounter anger and frustration; none of us is going to suddenly evolve beyond our everyday emotions. But you'll have a shared pathway to follow through the conflict and come out on the other side.

Follow up your organization's "advance understanding" conversation with a session that codifies the lessons you learned. When you put these lessons on paper, they can become your call in agreements. These agreements are your rules of engagement: the practices that everyone in the organization seeks to live up to whenever tensions rise.

Agreements should be short and memorable, and they can come in different forms. Some may focus on the attitudes your group promises to prioritize *before* conflict arises. Others focus on specific procedures for making it through conflict. Others still may specify what happens after a conflict ends. Here are examples of the call in agreements I come back to again and again:

When approaching conflict:

- Assume the best intentions.
- Grant each other permission to be imperfect.
- Bring a spirit of curiosity.
- Offer each other grace.
- Call each other in as often as possible.
- Build power *with*, not power *over*.

When conflict is underway:

- Avoid jargon and terms that make communication harder.
- Be honest about your emotions, but don't use them to shut another person up.
- If you're not in a positive headspace, postpone the conversation for another time.
- Don't just say your piece; listen actively and re-express what you hear.
- Know what outcome you're looking for. Do you need a specific change? Do you need to vent? Do you need to be heard?

When conflict is over:

- Maintain confidentiality: What happens here, stays here. What's learned here leaves here.

- If you hurt someone, acknowledge it, apologize, and make amends.
- If you debrief with someone else, don't gossip or exaggerate.
- Set a time for the *next* conversation.

Oops, Ouch, Whoa

Another model I love is a framework created by writer Annaliese Griffin: the "oops, ouch, whoa" model. Griffin's idea is to use those three keywords—"oops," "ouch," and "whoa"—to communicate how we're feeling throughout a difficult conversation.

As Griffin wrote:

> If you say something that comes out wrong, that you suddenly realize is kind of shitty, or just sounds different hanging in the air than it did in your head, you say, "Oops." If someone else says something that hits you in a way that feels bad, you say, "Ouch." If the conversation is moving too fast, you're not following a line of reasoning, you aren't familiar with a concept or an acronym, or you just want to slow down, you say, "Whoa," and ask for clarification.

The point is to signal a clear set of values: mistakes are normal, harm can be mended, it's okay to not know something, and accountability is a shared responsibility.

Griffin's model is brilliant because it gives us short, clear ways to express our feelings, allowing anyone to make themselves instantly understood. For environments where conversations might stray into sensitive subjects, I love the trust that the "oops, ouch, whoa" model enables. And I love that anyone can learn it in a flash.

Re-expression and Active Listening

One of the most common problems that call outs can cause is a constant feeling of threat. In an organization where call outs are common, you just don't know when you're about to set someone off. This can make it hard for us to speak up—and it can also make it hard to *listen*.

My favorite antidote is a strategy of *re-expression*. You can set ground rules for difficult conversations where, before we're allowed to criticize someone else, we have to *re-express* what they've said and give them a chance to respond. Say I hear a comment that strikes me as off-base. I would respond to the speaker by saying, "Here's what *I* just heard you say" and "Here's how it made me feel." I'm not straying into any kind of personal attack; I'm just focusing on the words themselves.

The point is to let the speaker have another chance to hear what they've said out loud—either as they'd intended it to be heard, or as it was misunderstood. They can then describe what they actually meant to say. Or they could apologize if they realize they indeed said something out of line.

Re-expression puts a few extra steps between a stray remark and the decision about how to respond. This alone can help defuse fraught situations and add clarity. Re-expression can also resurface points of agreement, as people discuss what they learned about each other's points of view. Often, we'll find that what seemed like violent disagreements are driven by unnoticed *violent agreements*.

For example, at SisterSong's national conference in Washington, DC, in 2009, some members wanted to support the campaign for

President Obama's Affordable Care Act with a spontaneous, unpermitted march to the Capitol. However, some conference participants were undocumented immigrants, and I had a fair understanding of the probable repercussions if we just led four hundred women of color toward the Capitol without a permit. While those of us who were citizens might get off lightly if arrested, the consequences for those without documentation could be severe. The debate became heated, but re-expression techniques helped my rowdier colleagues and I find what we could agree on.

In a call out culture, it's common for agreements to turn into arguments; re-expression helps turn conflicts back into conversations. We agreed we didn't want to leave DC without making a difference. So I proposed that instead of a march, we visit our congressional representatives without appointments, giving them no chance to hide. There's a tendency to assume that if two viewpoints aren't perfectly aligned, no progress can be made. But if we seek to identify what the different perspectives have in common and prioritize the points of agreement, it can still be possible to act as a powerful collective force. Most of the congresspeople we visited had never had four hundred women of color descend on them at one time, and we were delighted by how pleased many were to hear from women of color from their districts.

Here's another method for inserting a pause into a conversation before you jump in with criticism. When I was younger and in political study groups, we practiced a constructive approach called "self-criticism, criticism, and unity." We adopted a rule that we could only offer someone else feedback if we first publicly examined our own actions, responsibilities, and beliefs. The goal was again to put a barrier between ourselves and our knee-jerk criticisms. It helped us achieve cohesion and keep track not just of what we had in common but of the fact that everyone makes mistakes. When we couldn't go after someone else without putting our own actions and views under the microscope, it helped us all remain accountable through love and respect. Re-expression taps into a similar need to observe and develop a sensitivity to others' needs, so that we stay accountable to one another and the larger goals we're pursuing as a group.

Leadership in a Call In Culture

There are many ways to create a call in culture. Advance understanding and accountability allow you to establish collective buy-in, and to co-create an environment where people can work together, even across differences.

However, maintaining a call in culture also demands a special approach to leadership. When we move from a call out culture to a call in culture, we seek to embrace our ability to hold power *with* one another, not *over* one another. This approach requires avoiding a scarcity mindset as if there were limited power or attention that must be hoarded—but this can be difficult for longtime leaders to understand. "We currently live in a reality of scarce justice, scarce attention, scarce liberation," said adrienne maree brown. She encourages us to instead embrace an abundance mindset when we recognize that there's enough power and attention to go around.

Human rights advocates sometimes use a "take space/make space" approach to leadership, where the person who is the center of the conversation changes depending on circumstances. If we are talking about a fight against sterilization abuse, I'll feel qualified to take space and use my lived experiences to lead the discussion. If we're talking about immigration issues, however, I'll make space to let a more qualified person speak up. "Take space/make space" invites organizations to make the most of their collective knowledge and experience, and helps leaders and activists learn to apply their power where it is most effective—rather than clinging to hierarchy.

"Take space/make space" means knowing where the strengths and specialties of your team are. But it doesn't mean abdicating responsibility for or ignoring issues that don't center you. I can still use my power to play a role in all struggles—by working, for instance, to ensure that those who can lead are present and supported. And it *doesn't* mean thrusting the only Black person in the room into the spotlight whenever the subject of race comes up. Instead, leaders should create a space where everyone feels comfortable stepping up, if and when they have knowledge to offer. This lets us hear more voices. And it also lets us listen for what we're *not* hearing.

Paying close attention to who is quiet is a vital part of leading a call in culture. Power differentials may make it harder for employees to be candid unless extra reassurance is provided (and meant). You'll want to facilitate conversations in which people feel safe enough to voice their opinions. The goal is not the ideal of "safe spaces," which are unattainable, but rather "safe enough spaces," as Wesleyan University college president Michael Roth suggests. The concept of safety can be weaponized simply to shut down political opponents or forbid the teaching of subjects that deal with DEI (diversity, equity, and inclusion), race, gender, or any other topic that makes a complainant uncomfortable. It's important to distinguish between feeling unsafe and actually being unsafe. You can open up the floor with a simple call in prompt such as: "Would anyone else like to share their views?" Or you can invite the whole room in with a comment like: "I've noticed that most people aren't speaking up. Can we go around the circle and hear everyone's opinions?"

Leaders can even try offering what MIT economist Mary Rowe calls "micro-affirmations," which she defines as "apparently small acts, which are often ephemeral and hard-to-see, [. . .] which occur wherever people wish to help others to succeed." While a microaggression is a remark that pulls you out of a space where you feel you belong, a micro-affirmation preemptively affirms that you are where you need to be. Two students, for example, have told me that as first-generation college students, when professors or peers appreciate that they are fulfilling the dreams of their families, this type of verbal support helps address the isolation they sometimes feel. Other examples of micro-affirmations include trying to correctly pronounce everyone's name or including a new person in a group invitation to lunch.

Self-awareness is important when acting from a place of power. As managers, we should learn to strategically use our vulnerabilities to model how to call each other in. Don't be afraid to show your pain and challenges. And understand that you'll frequently work in settings of racial or gender illiteracy that will produce endless opportunities for conflicts. One trick to make having difficult conversations easier is to stop defining them as difficult. Instead, make them welcome, joyful, and enlightening. Another is to appreciate that call outs can provide you with useful information (perhaps through Slack or Twitter) that you'd otherwise have to pay a consultant thousands of dollars to obtain.

Calling In Those with More Power than You

Calling in is trickier when acting from a position without much power. If you're an employee seeking to bring up a microaggression or a recurrent issue to your boss, you'll be asking your higher-up to cede their control and ego for the course of the conversation, and that's something that may not come naturally to them. So it's best to schedule the time to talk in advance, and best to have the conversation one-on-one. If they're genuinely interested in changing their behavior, this will give them the time to absorb your feedback and reckon with the realization that they're not perfect—and not the boss—on every issue.

Trying a public call in—at an office-wide meeting, for instance—will be riskier. You'll make sure you're noticed, but you'll also be challenging your boss's sense of control in real-time, in front of others. This is a recipe for triggering their fight-or-flight reaction, which means they'll be sweating or seething instead of fully listening.

It's frustrating that calling in folks higher up the power ladder often requires extra care. But, pragmatically, we all hate to be publicly challenged, and there's an extra shock of embarrassment about being called in for anyone who thinks they're supposed to be in charge. It's better to let that shock discharge without hurting anyone. Even if it feels patently ridiculous as an entry-level employee to consider that your CEO might feel insecure over a slight misstep, it's the truth. Capitalism likes to pretend that a leader is one hundred times more valuable than any other person, but the reality is that they are just as human, just as vulnerable, and just as liable to respond with indignation or frustration.

Calling In as a Witness

When call outs occur, there is usually a sharp binary: one person is perceived as the victim and the other as the abuser. But others present can assist in analyzing and defusing the situation by serving as witnesses who help both sides understand the conflict and build common ground. Healers may be needed to validate people's emotions and help them understand the source of their feelings. Truth seekers can help investigate the facts under dispute. The decision about which role works best for you depends on your personal assessment of your emotional bandwidth at that particular time.

Maybe sometimes you're tempted to do nothing. To be polite. Because you don't want to cause problems. And besides, you're not the one who did wrong. So you remain uncomfortably quiet. That is your right. If you're not in a mental space to intervene constructively, it may be better that you don't try. But if you're just anxious to get involved, consider whether you may be causing a bigger problem by not saying anything. The problem with not standing up to injustice is that it normalizes it. It makes it seem that those who violate the human rights of others are not doing anything weird. A calling in mindset should make us braver and less likely to ignore the injustices around us.

When Your Organization Is in Crisis

Our internal conflicts often determine our external conflicts. Some call outs are not about particular people or their roles but systemic failures, yet they feel very personal to everyone involved.

Calling out can be particularly awful for many organizations on the right and the left. Believing we are the vanguard of radical consciousness, we can prioritize showing off our intellect or presumed higher morality, alienating one another in the pursuit of purity of opinions and nitpicking each other into grudging obedience or anxious silence. When internal problems arise, instead of strategically working with others to solve them, we may stage public call outs (usually through social media), perhaps even exaggerating how "abusive," "performative," "toxic," "woke," "transphobic," or "racist" the organizations—and the usually white, cisgender leadership—are.

I've heard from many leaders in corporate C-suites seeking assistance in such circumstances, mistakenly believing calling in is a quick fix. I generally advise them that if groups are at a crisis point, then conflict resolution and negotiation may be a more appropriate intervention. Calling in works on the assumption that people want to work well together but need more skills to do so. If they don't want to work together, you've got bigger problems. For example, I was once asked to facilitate a calling in training for an organization in the middle of "mission drift"; in other words, the organization was responding to pressures from funders that did not align with its values. While teaching calling in techniques could certainly have improved employees' ability to talk to one another, the fundamental problem would have remained. Without firm agreement on the purpose of the organization, an over-reliance on calling in techniques may have simply papered over significant disagreements rather than excavating what needed to be done to reset the organization's focus and priorities.

But what if your problem is more subtle? What if there are just one or two people who are continuing to call coworkers out or refusing to take accountability for their actions? You might be tempted to pull them aside to ask how you can support them as they try to change their behavior. And maybe this sort of quick intervention might help. But often, a better solution is to de-individuate the problem. People can only be as dysfunctional as an organization allows. To get to the root of the issue, you need to figure out the structural breaking point. Do you need better reparative processes? Better procedures to healthily deal with grievances?

How to Create a Call In Culture with Family and Friends

When I speak to people about calling in, the most common stories I hear in response are always tales of loss. An older white man might speak up first, then a twenty-something Black woman, both with tales of call outs that have cost them long-term friendships or family ties. They tell me about the relatives who were once close but who've stopped inviting them to holiday dinners, the friends who stopped texting months ago.

After Trump's 2016 victory, one Reuters/Ipsos poll found that "16 percent of respondents said they had stopped communicating with a friend or family member because of the election," as Joe Pinsker reported for the *Atlantic*. "Four years later, many such relationships are still in disrepair," he wrote.

I've found the same, and not just as a result of national politics. Any form of call out can have a brutal fallout.

Estranged relationships are painful. People want to connect again, but doing so feels terrifying. How do we reengage our loved ones when the wounds still feel so tender? And how do we prevent that pain from occurring again?

The first thing I tell people about calling in loved ones is something none of us want to hear: give up trying to change their minds. You can't keep trying to have the same conversation again and again while wondering why nothing is changing. And besides, it's not your place to manage their emotions or control how they feel. Instead, manage your expectations. Persuade them to *be in relationship* with you, not to *agree* with you. You might not bring them into your 90 percent circle, but you can at least help them from straying all the way to the 0 percent.

Mom and I didn't speak for several years after she sought to gain legal custody of my son, claiming I abandoned him while I was in college. In retrospect, she had her reasons: she wanted to get him health care coverage, as he wasn't included in Dad's military benefits. But I was enraged that she did this without telling me her plan or asking permission, because if the government thought I had abandoned my child, that could have lifelong repercussions. I stopped sending her Mother's Day cards since she was unwilling to acknowledge my motherhood. And Howard and I disappeared into the streets of Washington, DC. Keeping her wondering about our welfare was the worst punishment I could think of.

It was nearly a decade before we started to call on each other to be better together. My son was a teenager by then, and I began to understand the challenges she'd faced in raising a stubborn child like me. One night, I called her in desperation when Howard didn't return from an overnight trip with his high school swimming team. I was crying when I called her, fearful that she would lash out and tell me I was a bad mother. Instead, she laughed at the irony, calmed me down, and told me to go to bed. My son returned late the next morning; the school bus had broken down. He'd tried to call me several times but got a busy signal on my landline because I tied up the phone searching for him.

This incident helped tremendously in establishing adult-to-adult calling in conversations with Mom that became more respectful and less fractious over time. I learned to set boundaries and she, eventually, learned to honor them. We relied on our love for each other to trust we did not intend harm.

Many of us have recalcitrant relatives who require us to navigate bonds of family, patterns of harm, and our need for belonging and acceptance. After one of my online calling in trainings, a participant

I'll call Erica (a pseudonym) reported that she'd had the most transformative conversation with her mother-in-law in fifteen years. Since her mother-in-law is an avowed Trump-voting, Fox News–watching true believer, Erica despaired whether she would ever succeed in having a civil conversation with her. Even before politics became explosive, she'd endured years of belittling. Erica felt that her mother-in-law competed for her husband's affections and constantly criticized everything she thought and did.

Erica reported that she'd used a tactic for 50 percent allies on her mother-in-law. Instead of reacting to the hurtful words as she usually did, she paused and asked, "Why do you think I don't care about our family as much as you do? Tell me more about what you've been through that led you to make that assumption. I'd like to know more about how hard it was when you were raising kids, so I can learn from your experiences."

With these questions, Erica reported that the atmosphere between them changed, as they began to share exchanges about financial pressures, the difficulty of keeping children safe, and a host of other issues they had in common but had never previously discussed. Instead of dealing with the tip of the emotional iceberg, she dove underneath the water to see what was below and refocused the conversation on family values, shared worries, and the bedrock love they shared for Erica's husband.

"What I discovered," Erica wrote to me, "was that I didn't need a magic fact book to roll out and refute all her reasons. I was able to use the little knowledge I had and my basic humanity to discuss the issues. And we got somewhere!" This story affirmed for me that calling in techniques can help improve many relationships that once appeared beyond saving.

Another example I like to use is my uncle Frank (also a pseudonym). Many of us have an uncle Frank. He's a friendly and unassuming guy, except for one superpower: he can stop any dinner table conversation in its tracks by interjecting something racist, sexist, homophobic, or otherwise jaw-dropping. Uncle Frank generally said something outrageous to get attention because he enjoyed arguing. This time, in 1985, he was railing against "illegal aliens," claiming that Mexican immigrants should be stopped at the Texas border because they were accepting lower wages that undercut jobs for "real" Americans.

Tensions were historically high in San Antonio between African Americans and Chicanos. Anti-Mexican racism was encouraged by white business leaders, who used Black people as a buffer to keep Mexican Americans out of the economy. When I was growing up, signs read "No Mexicans/No Spanish" instead of "No Colored." We all learned the bunch of anti-Mexican slurs Uncle Frank was spewing.

In response to Uncle Frank's outbursts, everyone usually buried their face in their plates. When I attacked him, I became identified as the disrupter, the intolerant one who used political differences to weaken our family ties. No one else spoke up to defend people who weren't there, so all the family frustration landed on me, not Uncle Frank.

So this time, instead of angrily responding as I usually did as the family's "social justice warrior," I paused to calm myself. Then I turned to him. "Uncle Frank," I said, "you know I love you. I love your kindness, your sense of humor, and your love of family. If you could, I know you'd rush into a burning building to save someone regardless of their race, or whether they're gay or an immigrant. How can I reconcile this great Uncle Frank I love with the words you just said? Help me understand how that kind man I know you are is the same person who says things that can hurt people that you don't even know."

Instead of staying trapped in old patterns of interactions, I wanted to try something new. By assuring Uncle Frank of my love, I created a chance for him to recognize the dissonance between how good he thought he was and how he appeared to others. I didn't call him out, but I also didn't give him a pass on his bigotry just because he was family and I wanted to preserve an uneasy peace. By calling on him to do better, I offered him a chance to improve our relationship, with no risk that he would lose my affection.

This strategy does not guarantee more productive conversations. But it is often better than name-calling, which can quickly escalate into hurtful fights. And it modeled for my other family members how to stand up for others rather than letting hatred go unaddressed, sacrificing our moral integrity, and betraying our professed Christian values.

In my anger, I'd often wanted to kick Uncle Frank out of the family, although Mom would have never agreed to uninvite him to dinner. It wouldn't have worked anyway because I couldn't kick him out of my heart. There's a lot of talk these days about cutting people out of our lives, but I personally don't see family as disposable unless they are exceptionally toxic or dangerous to one's physical or mental health. They're the people I expect to see at weddings and funerals and all the family gatherings in between. These events don't need any added stress; there's usually enough already.

Uncle Frank didn't immediately answer my question, but I'm proud to report that he has never uttered another racist, anti-immigrant, or homophobic slur in my presence since that day. I can't control what he does at other times. And perhaps when I'm not around, he's also considering how others perceive him.

Here are three points that are helpful to keep in mind when calling in family and friends. (1) Don't respond directly to their words.

(2) Take a moment first to calm yourself. (3) Remind them of their inner goodness that you'd like to see more of. You can lay it on thick if that feels right for you, or you can keep it loving but brief. But don't reach for sarcasm. Let them *hear* the love and the genuine question—*How can both versions of you coexist?*—and they'll often begin to ask themselves the same thing. There are friends and family in my life who don't agree with me but who might have the same or similar values, which I'll only learn if I choose to ask questions instead of making assumptions.

It's often also helpful to make plans for your next conversation with family members and friends whom you're trying to weave back into your life. Maybe you might invite them to a one-on-one lunch date or a birthday party. Any opportunity to display family affection is useful to end the isolation of estrangement.

Of course, some folks delight in cruelty. While heart transplants are real, empathy transplants are not. I'm not naively suggesting that calling in strategies will work in every situation. But they offer a better chance of making progress with those who have inner kindness to build upon.

For the others, I reserve the right to call them out.

When It's Time to Call It Off

What do we do when calling in *doesn't* work . . . but nor do we think the other person deserves to experience the wrath of a call out? Even if you do everything right, you still might not find a receptive audience. The people you choose to call in have their own lives, dreams, and experiences, and change is neither easy nor quick. Calling in does not grant you the magic power to control others. It permits you to make a first overture, which can then grow step-by-step to become a change in trust, attitude, and—eventually—behavior. But you can never walk those steps for another person.

What's up to you is to make that initial offer. And really, your first decision should be *whether* it's likely to be worth it to call someone in. Each situation is different, but there are certainly warning signs that a call in is likely to fail. It's not the wisest strategy, for instance, to call in someone who can respond with punishments that materially affect your life. Think twice about when and how you call in someone who could evict you or—if your workplace doesn't yet have a robust call in culture—fire you. In such situations, it might be helpful to seek the guidance of others who have experienced similar dilemmas to develop another strategy for your protection.

What if you've tried to call someone in and they just refuse to accept it? Here are a few examples of how to recognize when an attempt at calling in has failed and it's time to spare your energy:

1. When the person has been offered a chance to reconsider their actions and impact on others but doesn't want to be accountable.

2. When a person is more concerned with gaining power through manipulating others, rather than being in community with others to build collective power.

3. When someone makes you feel unworthy and insists that you make yourself smaller so they don't feel intimidated by you.

4. When the person dismisses your bid for connection in favor of continuing the conflict.

5. When you are feeling activated or triggered and can recognize that you are no longer in a healthy head space to call in.

When the energy required to continue a call in conversation is more than you are now willing or able to expend, you may want to pivot to another of the 5Cs. You could be justified in switching to a call out if your counterpart continues to unapologetically cause others harm. You could call on the person to do better but acknowledge that you just don't have the time or the energy right now to help them down that path. But if the root of the conflict is minor—inappropriate language, rudeness, a personal insult—I would simply disengage. Others' negativity isn't worth my time and won't improve my happiness. And that's okay. Don't feel guilty. Calling it off is an essential part of our calling in tool kit—a way of preserving our energy so that we have the stamina for the fight ahead. Remember that there will always be an opportunity to call someone in another day. And there will be other ways to help to spread the values and principles of calling in far and wide.

Creating a Call In Culture on Campus

I've spent much of the past decade as a college professor, mostly teaching at colleges in Massachusetts (Hampshire College, Smith College, and a graduate course at Harvard University), with one year at Arizona State University in Tempe and a virtual appointment at Presidio Graduate School in San Francisco. Needless to say, there are vast cultural and political differences between each campus, especially between Arizona's Valley of the Sun and Massachusetts's Pioneer Valley.

But the needs of students are largely the same. They have been trained to perform according to testing standards and so desperately want to find the right answers to everything, which increases their fears of being wrong. They are hypersocial, sensitive to the opinions of their peers, and even more susceptible to groupthink than older adults. They mimic the extreme behaviors they find online, sometimes harming their fellow students because they don't appreciate the long-term consequences of their actions.

In the past decade, the Right has become obsessed with describing campuses as the depraved epicenter of cancel culture. They accuse educators of brainwashing students, which is hilarious because if I could brainwash them, I'd make them turn in their assignments on time!

But it's true there is a great deal of inspiring political energy on college campuses around the country. I learn as much from my students as I offer them. Their energy feels like sticking my finger into an intellectual socket because they always astonish me with their brilliance and compassion. The students in my classes remind me of the ones journalist Dashka Slater had in mind when she reported, "They don't want to be preached at or lectured to or spoon-fed—they want to be asked to think, to be exposed to new ideas and perspectives." They are so naturally optimistic and intersectional that I do not doubt that the world will be better in their hands.

But I've also seen plenty of destructive—or simply unfocused—call outs on campus. After swastikas were found on the walls of buildings at Smith in 2019 in an antisemitic hate crime, I found myself counseling students to keep focused on fighting the fascists instead of spending their precious energy blaming university leadership for not adequately defending them from the bigots. As the internet has made calling out a popular tool, I've heard students and faculty alike ask about how to steer that energy so that it less often descends into destructive call outs and moves more toward productive goals. This is a truly important question.

Students are in the process of learning. They are defining who they are, what is important to them, and how they want to live in and contribute to the world. They're new adults, exploring their power. And many have embraced radical ideas without having yet learned the radical skills to handle these ideas compassionately and inclusively.

This isn't a knock on anyone; it took me *decades* to learn these skills. And it required a lot of help from the mentors mentioned throughout this book.

Unfortunately, campus administrators and faculty are ill prepared to deal with the call out culture we live in. They tend to want to minimize incidents, so that bad news doesn't leak out to parents and donors. They may calculate that avoiding conflict is more beneficial than directly addressing it. Feeling frustrated and unheard, students may then escalate matters, causing even more uproar and pain on all sides. Sometimes, too much responsibility is devolved onto student leaders, who are also tasked with keeping the peace. These difficulties are often beyond their skill sets. In such situations, I find myself asking, "Who are the adults here? Why are we avoiding our responsibilities and requiring that students solve these problems?"

As professors and administrators on campus, our job is neither to baby students nor to punish them for trying to live up to their ideals. But we can make sure that they know there is an alternative to brutal call outs. We can help guide them to the ideals of calling in.

Here are three recommendations I often make to my fellow educators:

1. Don't fear your institution being called out. Call outs offer vital information. Often, controversies such as #Black at [your school] reveal hidden structures or patterns of injustice. Instead of fearing these eruptions, reframe them as opportunities to gather information visible to students but unknown to you. Learning this information offers the school's leaders a chance to change things that harm student learning environments.

2. Affirm students' right to challenge authority; it reinforces their critical thinking skills. Children raised in strict doctrinal households have their critical thinking skills suppressed at an early age. They are discouraged from seeking facts that may challenge their beliefs. Growing up under these restrictions means the brain structures that support critical thinking and logical reasoning don't fully mature. Learning to challenge authority is part of learning to trust their ability to form their own opinions.

3. Be honest and transparent about your reality. Some student demands are beyond your power to grant—and students deserve to know that—while others are within your power. Students can be taught the difference.

Students can, of course, also take these recommendations to heart. Within student groups, many of the call in agreements mentioned earlier in this chapter are easy to adopt. These can go a long way to turning potentially fearful environments into joyous ones. These same call in principles also apply to interactions between students and faculty.

Too often, I've seen divides build up on campus communities between faculty, administrators, and students—not to mention alumni, donors, and the board of trustees. Inevitably, students are going to have to work with people in positions of authority with whom they disagree. And faculty need to be able to educate students with whom they have differences. Yet there's a wall of fearfulness and distrust that is growing more common lately, even though all of these stakeholders have brilliant ideas and the abilities needed to make their community a better place. Just as within an organization, we need to think creatively about how to share power *with* one another, rather than trying to pin one another to the mat with demands for power *over*.

Today's students, faculty, and administrators are vulnerable. There are people whose political goals are to deform education to produce young people susceptible to manipulation to support an unjust status quo. Opponents of higher education do not want diverse campuses or students who think for themselves. While disguising their white supremacist motives as concern for colorblindness and fairness, they accuse colleges of foisting unqualified people of color or women into positions they have not earned. Calling in campus communities to stand together in defense of one another is part of the solution. Students must have opportunities to learn about free speech issues—such as the difference between offensive and assaultive speech—and to practice their leadership and collective action skills by learning how to balance sensitivity and the robust exchange of ideas. A high-quality education does not prevent the discussion of unpopular ideas or support the silencing of people who offer fact-based yet controversial views. But we should also remember that, according to *The Chronicle of Higher Education,* calls for greater freedom of speech on campuses, however well intentioned, risk undermining colleges' central purpose, namely, the production of expert knowledge and understanding. . . . Expertise requires freedom of speech, but it is the result of a process of winnowing and refinement that is premised on the understanding that not all opinions are equally valid. . . . The function of higher-ed institutions is not to mirror public opinion but to inform it.

An education should teach students how to question their beliefs, determine their stances on issues, challenge conformist groupthink, and grow in the knowledge vital to the functioning of a liberal democracy.

Inevitably, there are going to be issues where students demand more than administrators can offer, or where administrators are overly dismissive of students' concerns. A few years ago, I was asked to intervene on a campus where a donor had offered a multimillion-dollar gift to establish a new School of Public Health that would focus on health disparities created by poverty, medical racism, and disease. A controversy erupted after the donor publicly referred to the COVID pandemic as the "China virus" and students demanded that the university reject the donor's gift. They also requested university-wide sensitivity training with a particular emphasis on anti-Asian bigotry. Of course, rejecting a multimillion-dollar donation was never going to happen. Yet the students had a point about the pervasiveness of anti-Asian racism. Hate crimes against Asian Americans were dramatically increasing nationally during the pandemic.

Unfortunately, all the administration chose to do was to quickly hire a DEI consultant to do some basic sensitivity training—a worthwhile but incomplete endeavor. Done well, DEI can help people achieve the inclusion goals they desire. But done badly, it can build resentment and distrust. If it's done from a place of love, DEI work shows evenhanded and sincere concern for everyone, regardless of their identities. Done from a place of anger, it risks relying on identity essentialism, which can shame people for being who they are, often leaving the group worse off than before.

On this particular campus, this partial solution left many of the underlying issues—like the inability of each stakeholder group to civilly talk to each other without assuming the worst intentions—unaddressed to fester in the future. The university did not work to create a culture of trust, generosity of spirit, and healing across power differentials. That can was kicked down the field for someone else to stumble over later.

Even when a student call out might be "successful," it can often be a missed opportunity. I recently followed an incident where a white gay professor repeatedly used the word "nigger" while reading a poem that contained that slur. The students rightfully objected to this—it was unnecessary and insensitive for a white man to use the word in front of his class—and he was reassigned by the university. I wished a calling in approach had been used instead, as it would have provided a teachable moment for everyone: an opportunity to gain experience in how to effectively stand up for other marginalized groups. Instead, the university was embarrassed, the students lost the chance to learn from an award-winning professor, and the professor may still not understand that his sexual identity does not excuse him for casually using white supremacist language.

Calling in practices are fundamentally about learning, encouraging growth, curiosity, and a willingness to be challenged. They have a natural and important place on campuses. And they involve teachable skills that can be incorporated into the curriculum. Administrators and faculty need to recognize that calling in is an option—not always the easiest one but often the most effective.

University of Pennsylvania campus free speech expert Dr. Sigal R. Ben-Porath sees colleges as "laboratories in which democracy is learned, practiced, and enhanced" and where "Networks of trust and shared knowledge result when the typical mechanisms of inquiry—exchange of ideas, expertise, research—are paired with social complements—friendship, discussions across difference, civic engagement with the wider community." What better place to teach the next generation how to care for one another, stay tethered to the values we hold dearest, and believe in our ability to evolve and change?

Creating a Call In Culture at Large

You'll have noticed a paradox by now. Most of my strategies for calling in are focused on in-person conversations, happening within dedicated groups, and with the people we know. But many of the call outs and cancellations that attract the most attention in our culture occur online, often involving strangers, celebrities, or politicians. If we want to replace the larger call out culture with a call in culture, don't we need to know how to call in high-profile cases?

People often ask me: If I don't know a random internet influencer well enough to be in a place to call them in, what am I supposed to do? Let it go? And my answer may be unsatisfying to them, but it's simple: *Yes!* Let it go. If you don't know someone well enough to call them in, if they haven't directly harmed you, if you're not involved in the actual situation—then you shouldn't be calling them in *or* out. You're just adding noise.

Over the past decade, the call out culture has merged with the attention economy. The bar for what is profound has been lowered to what is entertaining. We see a tweet that Taylor Swift's fans have called out Beyoncé, and the Beyhive is coming for Swifties in response. We see a TikTok of some random convenience store clerk making a fool of themselves, and millions of people are already piling on. We see that another popular comedian has stepped past the line *again*.

It may feel like each of these mini-moments involves us because we can weigh in, amplify, and make a post of our own. But they don't really involve us. They call out for our attention, but they don't often require it. And it's up to us to step back and ask whether they're really deserving of our time and energy. Tweeting or shouting outrage is not the same as activism.

Remember how many moviegoers cosplayed the extravagant African-themed costumes of *Black Panther*? And yet when white people chose to dress themselves or their children in *Black Panther* costumes, Twitter erupted, accusing them of cultural appropriation. This made little sense to me. Dressing up for *Black Panther* is different from the mockery of wearing Indian headdresses as a Halloween costume or naming a sports team after a race of people. Understanding this nuanced difference is a sign of political maturity, like understanding the difference between blackface and liking jazz. Cultural theft is markedly different from cultural solidarity.

For 99 percent of public call outs, it's just not worth engaging. That's not to say you can't appreciate a viral news story for what it is: twenty-first-century popcorn. But don't think that everything that asks for your attention deserves it. The 1 percent exception are the justified call outs I discussed in chapter 2, the instances of true wrongdoing that have been ignored and will continue to cause serious harm if they aren't stopped. These are the big #MeToo-type moments when all the criteria for a constructive call out are met. When these erupt, feel empowered to enter the fray.

Save your attention and time for the problems that warrant it. Engage in a measured way with the conflicts and people you can realistically help, rather than shouting into the digital void. You'll realize that you're clearer and more focused. If a friend steps in it on social media—if they become Bean Dad 2.0—then you can certainly call them in. Hell, they'll probably welcome a little clarity and love—even tough love—from someone they know. But don't go searching for petty fights. When we do, that's what creates the bogeyman version of the call out culture. We see a culture of unforgivability that transfers from the internet to the personal sphere. And that's where it gets particularly damaging, where we lose all focus and lay into our friends and family as if we're engaged in an internet flame war.

I realize this advice may come as a letdown. Doing something is always so much more satisfying than doing nothing. But knowing when it's wise to call it off is every bit as essential for creating a global calling in culture as knowing when to call someone out or in.

We can regain our focus by starting close to home. That's why I choose to start in the personal sphere. Because building a call in culture—even one that's big enough and strong enough to replace the broader call out culture—needs to start with us and the ones we love. It starts in the places where we *can* make a difference. We want to spend our attention, our grace, and our forgiveness there, so that we can build better families, communities, and movements.

Once we start looking, there are opportunities for call ins everywhere in our daily lives, like standing in a supermarket checkout line or waiting at the Department of Motor Vehicles while renewing your driver's license. With people at the outer edges of your sphere of influence. It can be harder to engage in call ins in places like these, as there are no ground rules that encourage civil discussions. No one is pausing to establish rules of engagement. You're dealing with strangers, not people you know. And we're socialized into caring the most about the people who know us. This does not prepare us to easily extend our compassion to strangers. But in a universalized calling in culture, instead of only caring for a limited number of people, your integrity compels you to care for others the same way. So show patience to the rude customer or the weary DMV employee. Call them in, not out, when they're out of line. It's not just something to do for them. It's what you do for yourself. You'll feel better. And you'll model for others how to deal with unexpected drama.

Once we put calling in ideas into practice around us, it's not hard to transfer them to the culture at large. It may cost you a minor dopamine rush, but it keeps anger and hurt from spreading. At the heart of call in culture is that simple act of love.

8.

REDEMPTION AFTER A CALL IN

We all fuck up. All of us. I've called out and been called out plenty of
times. . . . But when we shut each other out, we make clubs of people
who are right and clubs of people who are wrong as if we are not
more complex than that, as if we are all knowing, as if we are perfect.
But in reality, we are just really scared. Scared that we will be next
to make a mistake. So we resort to pushing people out to distract
ourselves from the inevitability that we will cause someone hurt.

—Ngọc Loan Trần

***N**obody is perfect.*
    For most people, that's a platitude, the stuff of decorative
pillows and motivational posters. For me, it's an understatement: the
kind of line you hesitate to say out loud because you don't know how
much of yourself will spill out after it.

Let me take you back.

It's 1982 and I'm twenty-nine years old. I'm at the end of my third
year as director of the DC Rape Crisis Center, and I'm still visiting with
the Prisoners Against Rape. I've just joined Mayor Marion Barry's DC

Commission for Women; I'm its youngest member. I've co-organized the first historic National Conference on Violence Against Third World Women. And two years before, in 1980, I'd clawed out a six-figure settlement from A. H. Robins, the manufacturer of the defective Dalkon Shield IUD that sterilized me when I was twenty-three. Soon that victory will lead to a class-action lawsuit that vindicates hundreds of thousands of other sterilized women worldwide.

I was a young, rising political leader. I was making waves in movements at home, across the nation, and abroad. And I was doing it all as a single mother, a college dropout, and a survivor of sexual and reproductive abuse.

Hell, I was even generous with the money from my A. H. Robins settlement. I gave a chunk to my parents. I donated $20,000 to the Rape Crisis Center. I subsidized other activists' trips to the 1980 World Conference for Women in Copenhagen and helped fund a live-time broadcast back to the United States so women who couldn't attend could still participate. Only then did I put a down payment on a house and, yes, splurge on a fancy sports car.

I was doing it all. If you saw me, you would have seen a wunderkind.

But if you *really* saw me—saw past the exterior I was presenting—you would have seen my life was full of rot and wreck. I was doing it all *wrong*.

I had spent years seesawing between outright panic and suicidal depression because I'd still done nothing to deal with my childhood trauma. I was spreading myself thin, never getting enough sleep, racing between every commitment. Then, in November 1980, my friend Yulanda Ward was murdered in what we at the Rape Crisis Center believed was a politically motivated crime after twelve break-ins to our homes and offices. We didn't know who was targeting us, but her death shattered the last tether that had kept me grounded.

I drowned out my pain and insecurities with drugs. I became addicted to freebasing cocaine. Even as I self-medicated, I tried to hide my internal turmoil by throwing all my excess energy into political work, recommitting myself to the struggle despite the tremendous fears we all felt.

I remember foolishly bragging to my boyfriend that I'd never be broke again. It's a mercy he didn't laugh at me. But, within a few short years, I went from financially flush to entirely broke. I'd poured every last dollar into my drug habit.

At that point, I had a brilliant idea. I thought I could "borrow" back the money I had donated to the DC Rape Crisis Center. To my addicted brain, I'd be giving myself a temporary loan. But there was a more accurate term for it: *embezzling*. As the executive director, I ordered the bookkeeper to issue me money with no oversight or checks and balances. At least that's what I thought.

Fortunately, the center's board of directors caught on to my scheme almost immediately. I was forced to resign in disgrace. I still remember the headline blasted over the radio: "The Rape Crisis Center is in crisis!" It was my shame, shouted out on Howard University's radio station. When I heard it, I thought my feminist career—and, really, my life—was over.

What saved me were the Black women on the board of directors, and one in particular—Ama Saran. We both were single parents whose children were near in age, although she was about six years older than me. She'd become vice president of the board after Yulanda's assassination.

After the story exposed me, I hadn't wanted to see anyone. I didn't even want to leave my bed. I felt I was hanging on to the side of the world by my false fingernails. But when Ama ordered me out of hiding to attend my final board meeting, I was too broken and afraid to defy her.

I came to the meeting expecting to be flayed for my screwup, and rightfully so. But instead of calling me out, Ama called me in.

The first thing I remember her saying was that she was sorry for me. I had damaged my reputation and that of the Center, she said, but she was more confident that the Center would recover. She looked me in the eyes and told me that she knew I had more *potential* if I wanted to do better. She recognized my remorse and accepted my apology. She thanked me for showing up at the board meeting. She did not give up on insufferable me.

I don't know if I was even capable of making a sound then, but I must have told her that I did want to be better. I was nothing. I was a walking apology. But I wanted to be more again. I wanted to make up for everything.

Ama worked with me—publicly—to develop a reparations plan. I had to be held accountable. I sold my new car and house (at a loss, sigh) to restore the funds to the Center. Then she helped me find a therapist to address my trauma, and she offered the best political advice I'd ever received.

"Loretta," she said, "when you have bad news about yourself, be the first to tell it. Don't try to flee from it; don't fight it or deny it. Every other way the news comes out will be worse for you."

I did everything Ama told me. I saw that therapist, I repaid the Center, and I got clean. Every step was painful. For three years, I typed theses and dissertations for graduate students. Even after I'd cleaned up, I didn't think I could ever show my face again in a public-facing job in the national women's movement. I felt safer never talking about what I'd done.

During those years, I concentrated on international feminist solidarity work in South Africa, Latin America, and the Philippines. No one overseas knew my shame. Then, in 1985, I was hired at NOW. The organization didn't know the details of the scandal, and I wasn't yet up to confessing the story. I hoped that it had been forgotten.

But Ama wasn't done with me yet. In 1989, she recommended me for a job with Byllye Avery at the National Black Women's Health Project, helping me earn a shot at redemption in the Black feminist movement. It felt like coming home to the community I had betrayed.

It took me seven years to make that recovery, and it took me all that time to be able to tell anyone else about my embezzlement. I was still drenched in shame, well after I'd paid the Center back. Even now, part of me resists telling the details of this episode. But I'm publicly recounting the story in this book to share the important lessons I learned about accountability and second chances.

Ama Saran turned a call out into a call in when no one would have blamed her for piling on. I had shown her I was capable of grave harm, but in response, she showed me how to be capable of forgiveness, reparation, and redemption.

Her wisdom modeled a life lesson that saved my career and perhaps my life. There were nights, that first terrible year of my shame, when I would be driving home across the Woodrow Wilson Bridge in DC, and it took all my willpower to keep the steering wheel straight, instead of swerving off the bridge and ending it all.

I don't know where I would have ended up if Ama hadn't offered me grace. It's one of the most powerful actions I've witnessed and been lucky enough to learn from. And I believe that nearly everyone who has made a grievous mistake in the past should be extended the same opportunity for redemption.

I had not yet heard of notable civil rights lawyer Bryan Stevenson, but his words, discovered later, helped me understand what I learned from my public shame:

> There is a strength, a power even, in understanding brokenness, because embracing our brokenness creates a need and desire for mercy, and perhaps a corresponding need to show mercy. When you experience mercy, you learn things that are hard to learn otherwise.

The mercy Ama and Byllye granted me taught me more than I could have ever learned if my crime had been less shameful, and less visible. I was humbled and learned not to believe the hype about myself. But I also learned not to believe I was worthless just because I'd messed up so badly. That was the ultimate gift Ama offered me when she called me in—a chance to do better, not to give into despair.

She reminded me of what my mother said when she put me on the bus to Howard University in 1970: "Don't let success go to your head, and don't let failure go to your heart." I repeated these words like a mantra as I fought to piece together the shards of my dreams for myself and my son. To make a comeback; to have my suffering mean something; to make a life that mattered. I believed there was a point to my suffering, and while I couldn't always control what had happened to me, I could determine what I felt and did about it.

There's an ironic coda to this story. In 1992, I was asked to run for the presidency of NOW. I would have had the support of Ellie Smeal, and I knew the inner workings of the organization. But I confessed to the board members who'd approached me about running that I did not want my scandal to affect NOW—a scandal that they didn't know about (they'd somehow missed it, and Google wasn't available then for them to research me). I feared hostile anti-feminist forces would have exploited it to discredit an organization I deeply respected. It honestly felt like a weight was lifted from my soul when I was able to finally stop hiding that shameful secret.

Creating a Culture of Forgivability

What wrongs should we be held to account for? Which do we seek to punish? Which do we forgive? How long do we hold on to grievances, and how early in life do we begin to hold people responsible? The answers are not and never will be set in stone. They change over time, as should be obvious in a country that was built on a tradition of liberty boarded over a tradition of genocide and slavery. We are constantly negotiating which wrongs are *wrong*.

Today, there are crimes that we know are wrong, but there are also mistakes that we know are common, and that we know people can grow beyond. All of us should play back the tape recorder on our lives—what we thought, wrote, said, tweeted, and posted when we were kids, teenagers, and young people. We should self-assess whether we would pass the scrutiny that highly visible individuals such as Alexi McCammond have had to endure. Would we still have our jobs? Should people serve a life sentence of shame? Or could we live with a little extra doubt and a little extra stress for stray remarks or behaviors that no longer reflect who we are?

When someone admits a mistake, we have a choice. The key question should not be what they did when they were ignorant, but what they did when they had the chance to know better. One choice is about the past, the other is about the future. One choice slams an iron gate shut, while the other leaves a door of possibility cracked open.

Of course, the concept of forgiveness must be linked with accountability. Victims of racist violence in the Black community are constantly urged to forgive wrongs done to us for the sake of racial reconciliation. This rush to forgiveness denies people the right to be angry, to grieve, and to process the harm. We're supposed to be superhuman in suppressing our emotions. But healing and reconciliation cannot take place without truth and accountability first, without addressing the conditions and the feelings that caused the harm in the first place.

Still, forgiveness, when given freely, can be powerful. Although criticized by some Black people, the forgiveness offered by the victims of the 2015 Charleston massacre at Mother Emanuel Church was a statement of their dignity, courage, and humanity. As Chris Singleton, whose mother was murdered by white supremacist Dylann Roof, attested, "I've realized that forgiving is so much tougher than holding a grudge. . . . It takes a lot more courage to forgive than it does to say, 'I'm going to be upset about whatever forever.'" Forgiveness permitted Singleton to keep his power to bestow grace upon someone who'd hurt him tremendously.

Forgiveness is something you do for yourself before you can forgive others. Forgive yourself for when you knew you should've spoken up, but you were scared. When you spoke up for yourself and it didn't change things. When you judged others for their differences of opinion or experiences. By lacing our personal experiences with calling in theory and techniques, we can forgive ourselves for not being perfect.

I like to pre-confess my weaknesses so that they don't later bite me in the ass. I'm not seeking immunity but letting people know I'm a work in progress. I also ask people to consider why they are so critical of people who aren't the perfect people they secretly wish they could be themselves. It's as if people with flaws want to shame people for reflecting their own imperfections like a mirror. I've noticed that the people who are too quick to accuse others of theft, gossip, or lying are the ones most frequently guilty of those bad habits themselves. They judge people by what they would routinely do; it's a convenient tell when assessing people. Like my former colleague who religiously locked up the supply closet, but was later fired for stealing supplies herself.

Next, work on understanding forgiveness as a shareable practice. Understand your fear of feeling unforgiveable and commit to not making anyone else feel that way. We too frequently judge other people or groups by the worst examples of their behavior while going easy on ourselves because we know our good intentions. Honor them by acknowledging they are also a work in progress.

But in addition to learning how to forgive, we need to learn how to accept forgiveness. We've spent most of this book learning how to call others in, but it's also a skill to *be* called in, to apologize well, and to make the most of a second chance. Being called in is not a comfortable position to be in—even if, like me, you've found yourself in it enough times that it's no longer terrifying. It's a place of transition and decision, from which we can either choose to grow or dig ourselves in deeper.

I've been there, and I want to help. And so I'd like to more fully describe the steps that Ama Saran taught me: (1) acknowledge the harm, (2) apologize, (3) make amends, and (4) plan to prevent future harm. Following one or two of these steps can help, but with all four, redemption becomes a possibility, even in a culture of unforgivability. And by modeling how to be called in with grace, we can help to build a calling in culture.

How to Acknowledge the Harm

Whenever we're challenged out of the blue—corrected for our language, questioned for our assumptions, told we've hurt a friend—it's difficult to bear. Even when it comes from a place of love, we can find ourselves stewing in complicated emotions: indignation, embarrassment, fear, and a feeling of being trapped. "Finding the truth in a painful criticism is an exercise in self-discipline," writer Walter Rhein observed. "First you have to overcome your defensive response, then you have to overcome the reflex to reject things you don't understand. Both of these impulses are very powerful, and they can be deployed to derail productive discussions before they even begin." The most common response is to react with anger, fighting back against the perceived challenge. We may search for allies and confirmation of our good character, seeking to settle on a version of the story where we've done nothing wrong.

So, just as when we're calling in someone, we want to begin by taking a moment to pause, and breathe, and let those emotions settle. Call yourself in. Don't let your first reaction overtake you. Ask yourself: Am I showing up with defensiveness? Is that an indicator of another emotion, such as shame or guilt? Do I understand the problem? Do I hear what the other person is saying, even if I disagree?

Try to survey your behavior as if it were someone else's, as if you weren't aware of your own (presumably good) intentions. There is always a gap between what I've said and how it's received, and sometimes I must swallow my pride to acknowledge that the gap has become a chasm. When I'm called in, a question I like to ask myself is: "Have I done something that *could* have made someone else uncomfortable?" That seems like an obvious question, perhaps. But consider what I'm not asking. I'm not letting myself ask: "Did I really do anything *that* bad?" If I was called out rather than in, I'm *not* asking: "Do they need to be *so* angry in response?" It's *not*: "Don't I deserve a call in for this, instead of a messy call out?" It's *not*: "Does my *minor* wrong really deserve such a *serious* response?"

Questions like these are what make conflicts escalate. It's tempting for a person to create a wedge out of their indignation and claim that their anger is righteous.

Instead, you need to start by acknowledging the hurt and pain you have caused. You need to assume responsibility for what you've said and done, *even* if it wasn't intended, and *even* if you suspect the other person is overreacting. You can assume the other person is acting in good faith, just as you are—until and unless it's proven otherwise. If both of you are leaping right to your worst conclusions, you're just going to have a messy fight on your hands.

If you find yourself resisting—if you find your anger rising back up—try to settle for something easier instead. You don't need to start by acknowledging exactly *what* you've done, or even *that* you've done something wrong. Just acknowledge that you *might* have. That starting point should be enough to prevent an initial explosion, allowing for a conversation. From there, you'll be able to learn the other person's perspective and understand what went wrong from their point of view—which makes acknowledging your actions and apologizing a lot easier to consider.

How to Apologize—The Right Way and Right Away

When you're called out, there are two types of apologies you should have in your quiver. There's the "right away" apology, and the "right way" apology. Both do different things, and one doesn't preclude the other. In fact, many call outs, especially in-person conflicts, warrant *both*.

The "right away" apology comes early on in the conversation, right after I've acknowledged that I may well have hurt someone, but often before I've fully absorbed the whole situation. This apology often opens the door to an honest and unguarded conversation where I can learn more by listening. The "right way" apology comes later, once I've learned what I've done wrong—and internalized it to the point where I can offer my sincere regrets to the other person.

Why two types of apology? Because everyone *wants* the sincere, "right way" apology; but sometimes it takes a little while to get there, and we need a way of building trust in the meantime. The "right away" apology fills that gap.

First, thank the person, sincerely, for bringing this matter to your attention. Tell them you heard them and are going to give what they said some thought. This signals your willingness to receive feedback. Most people want reassurance that their opinions matter and will be heard.

I don't even have to believe I'm in the wrong to deliver my "right away" apology. At the very least, I can apologize for the impact of what I've done, even if that wasn't my intent. It's not about flagellating myself in front of people but about recognizing that I might have an opportunity to learn something. With a "right away" apology, I like simple and direct phrases: "I'm sorry I said that" or "I'm sorry I hurt you," ways of owning my actions and acknowledging harm. Direct options fare better than conditional apologies such as: "I'm sorry *if* I offended you," or "I'm sorry *if* I messed up." Both these alternatives suggest, however subtly, that *I* didn't do anything, and that it's *you* who are over-reacting. They only make your counterpart double down on criticizing you and justifying their own reactions. They raise tensions, whereas the purpose of a "right away" apology is to reduce them.

Note that you have not promised either a timetable or that you will agree with their assessment of the situation. You still get to decide what your response will be after you've had time to think about it.

Once I've delivered my "right away" apology, my goal is to engage in a conversation where I can listen openly and actively. I try to remember that this person has given me their attention and time, which I can try to learn from. If I become defensive, I won't help anyone understand me any better, *nor* will I learn their perspective on what I'm doing wrong.

My next step, if I don't understand what I've done wrong, is to ask for clarification, with questions like: "Do you have the time to help me understand?" This signifies that I *want* to learn how to do better, without presuming that the other person owes me an explanation and an education. It also helps depersonalize the conversation. We can then talk about which words, ideas, and actions are better options for the future. That's more productive—and less vexing—than debating back and forth about whether I'm simply a bad, wrong, and problematic person.

You might also ask how the other person is doing, how they were harmed by what you did or said, and if you could talk about your relationship. If they could have brought the presumed problem to your attention in a less dramatic way—if they called you out rather than in—that may indicate that they're feeling unheard or injured. By asking about them and their needs—by calling *them* in—you've invited them into a conversation instead of a conflict.

If you're part of an organization, you might discuss the art of making apologies before the need arises: When are they needed? What sorts feel insincere? How are they overused? What should happen when an apology is not offered? How many times should a person need to apologize?

If the "right away" apology opens the door to a productive conversation, then the "right way" apology is how we seek to close it once we've learned what it is that we did wrong and how we can improve in the future. Sometimes, I can only learn this through research and study *after* an initial confrontation. The mark of a sincere apology is to then *reflect* that learning back to the other person if you have the opportunity.

If I'm going to close out a calling in conversation with a meaningful apology, I want to be able to show the other person that I now understand (1) *how they feel* hurt, and (2) *what I did* to cause that wound. A "right way" apology always involves taking responsibility for both ingredients.

We're not trying to make *excuses* for what we did. That's often where our mind wants to go first: we want to insist that there's a clear explanation. That it was a mistake, or a fluke, or a funny story! But be wary of that instinct. If you can sum up your explanation quickly, it's okay to fit it in—but do *not* dwell on it. Even a justified explanation turns the attention to *you* rather than your counterpart. And with any apology, you have two more important priorities: to show the other person that you recognize *their* hurt and to show them that you won't let it happen again. You can accomplish both without getting caught up in self-justifying explanations. A "right way" apology prioritizes the other person's harm over your own reasons—good or bad—for causing it.

The only way to offer a sincere apology for something you've done is to change your motives. If you're still invested in avoiding embarrassment or winning an argument, your apology will be forced and insincere because you're still convinced of the rightness of your position. Don't over-apologize either, assuming a feigned responsibility for things beyond your control.

For some conflicts, like basic misunderstandings or interpersonal disagreements, a "right way" apology can be all it takes to bring people back together. If I used an outdated phrase and didn't know any better, maybe someone more in the know called me in. And if I've learned, apologized, and committed to avoiding the same language in the future, we can move on—to bigger and better goals.

When I listen to the profound wisdom of younger activists, no one explains the importance of making an apology to achieve accountability better than disability and transformative justice activist Mia Mingus: "True accountability is not only apologizing, understanding the impact your actions have caused on yourself and others, making amends or reparations to the harmed parties, but most importantly, true accountability is changing your behavior so that the harm, violence, abuse does not happen again."

But I should warn you that just because you've offered an apology doesn't give you the power to determine if the other person will accept it. And even if they do, for other conflicts—where you've inflicted more harm—we'll need a couple more steps to achieve anything resembling redemption. Apologies, after all, do not balance the scales of justice. They don't heal wounds, or wind back the clock. Apologies help us achieve forgiveness, which is important and necessary. But forgiveness is still distinct from justice.

How to Make Amends

Our society has witnessed too many instances of people fumbling the ball when their mistakes are exposed. They double down or claim that their sense of injury outweighs the injury they caused. Using a passive voice, they claim that "mistakes were made" instead of simply saying, "I made a mistake." Some people end up making a full heel-turn, embracing the negative attention and firing back at critics until they resemble cartoonish villains. Other victims of internet pile-ons dig themselves into deep holes because they decide to post through it rather than take time to reflect.

It always strikes me as such a strange choice to make. Because I don't think it ever needs to go that far. Our society might like to gawk at a villain for a bit, but what we really adore are the comebacks—the people who express their regrets, seek forgiveness, and turn their fortunes around.

It can seem humiliating to feel belittled and seek forgiveness. It can feel humiliating to *have* to make a comeback. But humiliation is never permanent, and forgiveness is almost always possible. *Especially* if you commit to making reparations for the wrongs you've committed.

When I took money away from the DC Rape Crisis Center, an apology was not enough. I had deprived victims of potential resources. If I'd simply let that stand, I'd be walking away as an exploiter of all those women who counted on me (not to mention, a criminal). When we commit harm that's serious enough to stay on the ledger, we need to be conscious of *reversing* that harm. Or else we're continuing to let the injustice stand.

In my case, it was possible to undo the damage; I could repay the lost funds and then some. But it gets harder to make amends when the damage is irreversible or difficult to define. For many types of harm—from physical to emotional, broken relationships to shattered trust—it is unclear what proper amends look like. This can throw us toward two extremes: where we act as if either no effort is *necessary* to make up for the harm, or as if no effort could *possibly* be enough to make up for the harm. The former is a culture of insensitivity and impunity, while the latter is cancel culture, where every harm has no solution but punishment. The better answer lies somewhere in between these extremes.

So how do we go about making amends?

The simplest way to begin to make amends is to ask how. Once you know you've wronged someone, ask if there's a way for you to do right by them. Most of the time, all they're looking for is an acknowlededgment and an apology, but if the harm is significant enough, there might be something else you can do. If you hurt someone physically, after all, it's not out of line for them to ask you to pay their medical bills. I've talked to people who ended up initiating lawsuits that could have been prevented if the person who'd harmed them had simply admitted fault and worked to make them whole. Sometimes, people just want to know no one thinks they deserve what happened to them.

For minor conflicts, you can consider getting creative: If you've taken up someone's whole morning because they were explaining "intersectionality" to you, you might offset it by offering to buy them lunch (if you haven't already exhausted their patience). If your aunt keeps misgendering her nephew, but she wants to do better, you might have a book in mind that you ask her to read. These are intangible amends—just enough to go beyond a simple sorry or a simple thank-you—and they work best with people we know.

In more fraught situations, where trust has been frayed, you might need additional help. If you know that amends are warranted but it's clear that you and the other party aren't on great terms, you could consider inviting in a trusted third party—perhaps a mutual friend. They could then weigh the situation and determine what the right amends would look like. That third party though needs to have the trust of both sides—or else the conflict can easily just spread further.

Amends are most important in situations where there's a clear injustice and the offending party has significantly more power than their counterpart. If a company is called out for racist hiring practices, for instance, or if an executive has been playing favorites, then the institution should be making amends that right the wrong and create an environment where it doesn't happen again. These can involve revamping hiring practices and adding new, qualified employees of color. Sometimes it means a donation to relevant causes that seek to redress the injustice on a larger scale. Sometimes it means firing executives who've had multiple chances, or adding new training measures, or revamping whole departments or business models.

Each of these measures can be effective if enacted with purpose. But they can also be mere window-dressing. The amends need to provide restitution for the initial wrong and those harmed by it—not simply divert attention and cover up internal rot. Because that rot just spreads, especially if we don't address it with one final step: planning to prevent *future* harm.

How to Prevent Future Harm

Recently, I was approached for advice by a woman of color who had started a very successful cosmetics business. She had built the company in just five years, and it had achieved more than $5 million in annual revenues. But she'd had to step down as its CEO after years of call outs and tensions within the company had gone unresolved. Some of her staff perceived her as too driven, too unfriendly, and too insensitive. They didn't feel involved in the company's major decisions—even many of the top executives. By the end, a string of relatively minor mistakes ended up growing into a collective discontent that pushed the woman out of her own company.

In talking to the CEO, I learned that one of the earliest issues was that she did not prioritize developing talent as the company was coming into its own. And she didn't have enough young people and people of color in leadership roles, an issue that was particularly relevant given the cosmetics products the company was selling. Critics called her out for this fact, and she panicked, committing a mistake that would only be amplified in the years to come. She responded by apologizing and trying to make amends. She quickly hired qualified young people and people of color for important roles, and she fully invested in their training. These were strong steps. But she made them reactively, out of her fear of being called racist or ageist. And she didn't take the time to determine where the original wrong had come from, or, crucially, how to prevent it in the future.

The CEO had patched up the public relations problem . . . until most of the new hires left after only brief stints. Her problem was not attracting people, it turned out, but keeping them. And it all stemmed from the same problem she'd started with.

When I asked her how she felt about power, or more specifically, about power sharing, I saw the truth that had dawned on everyone who'd worked under her. She revealed that her anxiety over the company's success meant she micromanaged every detail of her operations. She worked untenably long hours seven days a week and communicated that expectation to her staff, if not through words, then by example. Her ideal employee was someone who put in the same energy, who would treat the company as if they also owned it. But, at the same time, she wouldn't *let* anyone else feel like they could own the business. It was her baby, and she made sure each important decision was hers alone.

Eventually, her most talented people burned themselves out and left, until she was leading a staff of people who had less initiative and commitment. This increased her frustration, and she began to dislike the people she worked with. She ultimately chose to step down rather than continue to grind along with people she no longer trusted and who no longer trusted her.

When this CEO contacted me, she was trying to understand what had gone wrong, wondering if she dared to start a new business that might risk the same outcome. For her, I thought that risk was real because she hadn't ever gotten to the final stage of achieving redemption: She *still* needed to create a concerted plan to prevent the same issues from arising in the future.

That was her biggest error—and the most critical thing she would need to correct if she ever tried again. She had made fixes that looked functional, but they papered over flaws rather than addressing the real issue. If she was going to succeed, she would need to work on *that* problem first: her inability to share power.

I like this example because many people see the four steps to redemption and think that the fourth step—preventing future harm—is the easiest one. Once we've made our mistakes, sought to learn, apologized, and made amends, how could we even make the same errors again? Haven't we already learned, painfully, not to make the same mistake twice?

Take it from someone who's made the same mistakes again and again and again before learning from them: It's easier said than done. Because you can only avoid those same mistakes if you do the work to understand where they really came from. A lot of the time, we do exactly what the CEO did. We fix the surface-level issue without looking deeper into ourselves, where the more important fixes lie.

So what should we do? We work on ourselves, of course. That's where our plan for doing better needs to start. Take my own 1982 crisis: if I came out of that final board meeting and told you I'd learned my lesson, and that my lesson was simply not to embezzle again, you'd tell me that I was off my gourd. The world was teaching me a much larger lesson and a much more intimate lesson at the same time: I needed to focus on the battles I was still fighting within myself, to come to terms with my own pain and trauma, to forgive myself for not being perfect rather than bottling it all up and lashing out. I'd been advising rape victims to seek counseling and yet I hadn't taken my own advice. The world was telling me that the cycle could only end with me if I learned to spare a little bit of grace for my own struggles.

We start with ourselves, and we end with ourselves. That's the funny loop of calling in. Because when we forgive ourselves, we can find that forgiveness for others. Because when we grow within ourselves, we create a place where others can grow. Because when we cultivate our spark of joy, we can pass it along. Because when we live up to our values, we show others what beautiful lives can be possible.

So, what will you focus your attention on? The pain, the punishment, or the potential for healing and growth?

EPILOGUE

Letting Go of Hate

Don't ask what the world needs. Ask what makes you come alive, and go do it. Because what the world needs is people who have come alive.

—Rev. Howard Thurman

've never been that terribly invested in hating white supremacists or misogynists or opponents of reproductive justice or other folks who piss me off. Fighting them was a mission, but I didn't emotionally invest in actively hating folks I didn't even know. I've had awful things happen to me, but I was too forward-focused to work up the energy to actively hate my tormentors. Survival took all my energy. Or perhaps I was just too self-absorbed?

I've often wondered what people get out of all-consuming hate. It seems to motivate them in ways I find simply exhausting. Perhaps their hate provides a centering, a reason to get up every day, to do things. I don't know because even entertaining that type of motivation fatigues me. It seems like a lot of botheration for little return on investment. Like drinking poison and hoping the other person dies, as I believe Nelson Mandela said.

Dr. King said, "If we are arrested every day, if we are exploited every day, if we are trampled over every day, don't ever let anyone pull you so low as to hate them. We must use the weapon of love. We must have compassion and understanding for those who hate us. We must realize so many people are taught to hate us that they are not totally responsible for their hate. But we stand in life at midnight; we are always on the threshold of a new dawn." Each new day, I try to choose authenticity over perfectionism. I try to choose joy. I try to choose love.

I believe that the one human right that can never be taken away is the right to choose our own attitude, no matter the circumstances in which we find ourselves. I want to be known as someone with empathy but also high standards and expectations—of myself and others. I want to be seen as hardworking, direct, motivated, honest, clear, and passionate. What choices can I make each day to align my actions with these values? I also want to be seen as a person with faults, someone who does not always say the right thing or know the right answers. I'm not a good candidate for hand-holding or sugarcoating the truth, although these can be necessary skills in movement-building work; they are not my strengths but I'm working on becoming better.

I've never learned how not to be afraid—how not to listen to the interior chatter from my trauma that's never right but never stops. But I have learned how not to let my fear hold me back from trying to make the world a better place. I had to call in my heart and my backbone to stand up to my nightmares, to learn the compassion and joy I wanted to center in my soul. When I did, I found I had more strength and love than I knew. And I found my purpose in life by offering this blessing of joy and peace to anyone willing to listen, especially those whom I never expected to ever reach.

We can all do this: call ourselves in to call others in. I'm not special, and I'm sure not naturally extroverted. My best friends have always been books. Someone once said they think of their home as a library that just happens to have a kitchen, bedrooms, and bathrooms attached. That's me to a T.

Calling in techniques are not magical incantations, and they're not difficult to learn. The magic is how they affect you and those in your spheres of influence. I've been awed by what happens when I tell my truths. And I've learned that when I serve my people, my every dream will come true. I hope it works out like that for you as well.

Some of my greatest pleasures over the years have been the conversations I've had—the difficult ones as much as the joyful ones. The more consistently we call ourselves in, the more we learn to enjoy the learning we are gifted from others. If you are peacefully aligned with your values, you can talk to anyone and take joy in the messiness of us all stumbling through being human together.

ACKNOWLEDGMENTS

I dedicate this book first to my late parents, Lorene Deloris Burton Ward Ross and Alexander Elijah Ross. They were wonderful role models whose wisdom I'm just now fully appreciating. I can only offer them posthumous gratitude for the difficult task of raising this raucous child. Dad just calmly rolled with my organic raunchiness, but when Mom (and it was always Mom) said something that could stimulate my teenage rebelliousness, we generally ended up immersed in the call out culture. We eventually learned to call on each other to love better. I didn't know to name these choices calling in behaviors before she passed, but I appreciate that, before it was too late, we learned it was more important to love each other than win arguments. I wish I could show her this book. She was always proud of her children no matter how challenging we were.

I also want to honor my late son, Howard Michael Ross, who taught me the power of calling in by living a life based on paying it forward. As the son of an immature teen mother, he grew into an honorable man despite me, not because of me. He also did not live to see this book published, but I am who I am because he was who he was: a beloved reason to keep fighting against the odds. He gifted me with a fabulously brilliant grandson, Tristan Brown-Ross, and I hope this book makes him as proud as the title "Grandma" makes me.

Many others contributed uniquely to my thinking about the radical love of calling in through comments, conferences, and sharing articles. I list them alphabetically because I can't organize the list by the value of their contributions and importance in my life. It took more than a village to produce this book; it took a megalopolis. All errors are mine, and each person was helpful in a unique way. Some may be surprised to find themselves on this list, but their wise words and generous encouragement constantly inspired me to continue to believe in this project.

They are: Laurie Abraham, Katherine Acey, Mary Anne Adams, Alicia Afrah-Boateng, Asam Ahmad, Eyananda Ahmed, Julie Akeret, Bushwa Alawie, Rebecca Alvara, Ellice Amanna, Tatiana Apandi Anacki, Chris Anderson, Kelly Anderson, Lauren Anderson, Abdullahi An-Na'im, Lisa Armstrong, Margot Audero, Byllye Avery, Moya Bailey, Carrie Baker, Justin Baldoni, Emily Bellanca, Javiera Benavente, Jessica Bennett, Liz Bewess, Michaelann Bewess, Christina Bobel, Elizabeth Bohnel, Toni Bond, Margaret Bresnahan, Jose Bright, Laken Brooks, Bliss Broyard, Darcy Buerkle, Marianne Bullock, Linda Burnham, Pamela Wynn Butler, Jean Caiani, Ginetta Candelario, Matilda Rose Cantwell, Elizaeth Cardona, Maria Cartagena, Margaret Cerullo, Brittany Charlton, Floyd Cheung, Shakil Choudhury, Marc Chouinard, Jeanne Clark, Lauren Clarke, Jon Cox, Christa Craven, Kimberlé Crenshaw, Katherine Cross, Rosanna Cruz, Carrie Cuthbert, Vanessa Daniel, Annahid Dashtgard, Marian Davis, Tobias Davis, Roshanda Degraffenreid, Mike DeJoie, Tony DeMartino, Latrina L. Denson, Abigail Disney, Dázon Dixon Diallo, Deanna Dixon, Ejeris Dixon, Sonja Dolinsek, Ellen Dorsey, Lauren Duncan, Estelle Ellison, Kara Fagan, Kenyon Farrow, Joyce Follet, Lisa Fontes, Chiara Forrester, Raven Fowlkes-Witten, Janet Freedman, Marlene Gerber Fried, Liz Friedman, Alicia Garza, Kate Geis, Michael Gorra,

Acknowledgments

Suzanne Gottschang, Sara Gould, Marissa Graciosa, Adam Grant, Ryan Grim, Jennifer Guglielmo, Christian Gunderman, Corey Hajim, Kia Hall, Marcella Hall, Dwight Hamilton, Jennifer Hamilton, Desiree Hammond, Reilly Haran, Dan Harris, Kristen Helmer, Helen Hicks, Megan Hogan, Anna Holley, Lisa Huebner, Ajowa Ifateyo, Stanlie James, Jallicia Jolly, Hannah Joseph, Max Joseph, Valerie Joseph, Frank Joyce, Natalia Kanem, Jonathan Karp, Deborah Keisch, Stephanie Jo Kent, Shirley Kimbel, Shulamith Koenig, David Kuhn, Fhrynee Lambert, Daphne Lamothe, Carrie Lee Lancaster, Queen Lanier, Olivia Lawrence-Weilman, Ricci Joy Levy, Monica Lewinsky, Kristen Loken, Laura Lovett, Robynne Lucas, Fran Luck, Kristen Luschen, Anya Malley, Janet Marquardt, Beth Mattison, Vanessa Martinez, Amanda Major, Kathleen McCartney, Carolyn McDaniel, Carson McGrath, Alexandra McGregor, Dani McLain, Amy Medeiros, Bekezela Mguni, Noa Milman, Mia Mingus, Enrique Morales-Diaz, Mona Lisa Moualiem, Nate Muscato, Scot Nakagawa, Ruth Nemzoff, Paula Nikolaidis, Trevor Noah, Judy Norsigian, Suzanne Nossel, Jacqueline Novogratz, Jeannie Ochterski, Laurie O'Connell, Peggy O'Neill, Cara Page, Priscilla Painton, Jennifer Parker, Willie Parker, Jishava Patel, Cindy Pearson, Tonya Pearson, Suzanne Pharr, Josie Pinto, Sayra Owens Pinto, Karen Pittelman, Marisa Pizii, Andrea Plaid, Stephanie Poggi, Katha Pollitt, john a. powell, Elizabeth Pryor, Muneer Panjwani, Dani Planer, Stickli Quest, Anne Radecki, Freda Raitelu, Jennifer Rajchel, Grace Ramsey, Shannan Reaze, Sherrill Redmon, Walter Rhein, L'Tanya Richmond, Marian Rivera, Monique Ashley Roberts, Stuart Roberts, Arlene Rodriguez, Luz Rodriguez, Jamala Rogers, Nayiree Roubinian, Jeanine Rusham, Alina Ortiz Salvatierra, Kathy Sanchez, Jen Sandler, Ama Saran, Joshua Wolf Schenck, Beth Schiff, Stacey Schmeidel, Michael Schulder, Mab Segrest, John Selders,

Acknowledgments

Amilcar Shabazz, Sarah Shannon, Beverly Guy Sheftall, Alexis Shotwell, Aishah Shahidah Simmons, Monica Simpson, Alice Skenandore, Eleanor Smeal, Joshua Sparrow, Kathy Spillar, Jeremy Adam Smith, Mistinguette Smith, Tessa Smith, Hannah R. Sokoloff, Rickie Solinger, Zachary Stein, Gloria Steinem, Karen Stephen, Andrea Stone, Dominique Straugh-Turner, Rachael Strickler, Banu Subramaniam, Mia Sullivan, Diana Sutton-Fernandez, Norma Swenson, Sarah Swenson, Shira Tarrant, Sonya Renee Taylor, Sara Rose Testman, Karen Thurston, Christopher Tinson, Angie M. Tissi, Rosalie Toupin, Nkenge Touré, Marya Torrez, Ngọc Loan Trần, Lucy Trainor, Chloé Valdary, Marjorie Valdivia, Adrienne van der Valk, Akil Vicks, Rev. C.T. Vivian, Eric Ward, Maggie Webb, Greg White, Faye Williams, Juanita Williams, Angie Willey, Sarah Willie-LeBreton, Jamia Wilson, Tim Wise, Gabriella Wood, Rich Yeselson, Rachel Yousman, Jamil Zaki, Ziqi Zhen, Stella Zine, and Haley Zorn.

NOTES

Prologue

1   *"In the course of"*: Wangari Maathai, "Nobel Lecture," Oslo City Hall, Oslo, Norway, December 10, 2004.

1. How I Learned to Call In

9   *"I know the world is"*: Toni Morrison, "No Place for Self-Pity, No Room for Fear," *Nation*, March 23, 2015, https://www.thenation .com/article/archive/no-place-self-pity-no-room-fear/.

27   *"The practice of compassionate"*: Personal communication to author through email, July 23, 2023.

29   *"Anybody can become angry"*: Aristotle, *Nicomachean Ethics*, trans. W. D. Ross (Oxford: Clarendon Press, 1925; Internet Classics Archive, n.d.), bk. 2, https://classics.mit.edu/Aristotle/nicomachaen .html.

30   *"I picture 'Calling In' as a"*: Ngọc Loan Trần, "Calling In: A Less Disposable Way of Holding Each Other Accountable," December 13, 2013, BGD: Black Girl Dangerous, https://www.bgdblog.org/2013 /12/calling-less-disposable-way-holding-accountable/.

31   *Calling in is a philosophy*: Dr. Martin Luther King Jr., "We Need an Economic Bill of Rights," *Look*, 1968 (speech published posthumously), https://www.theguardian.com/commentisfree/2018 /apr/04/martin-luther-king-jr--economic-bill-of-rights?mc_cid =b3556c3e04&mc_eid=3672f86bbd.

31   *"let's turn to each other"*: "Civil Rights Leader Dr. Joseph Lowery Speaks Here Aug. 27," *Chattanoogan.com*, August 12, 2006, https:// www.chattanoogan.com/2006/8/12/90847/Civil-Rights-Leader -Dr.-Joseph-Lowery.aspx.

32   *As expert movement*: Kelly Hayes and Mariame Kaba, "How Much Discomfort Is the Whole World Worth?," *Boston Review*,

September 6, 2023, https://www.bostonreview.net/articles/how
-much-discomfort-is-the-whole-world-worth.

33   *As Audre Lorde recognizes:* Audre Lorde, *A Burst of Light* (Ithaca, NY:
        Firebrand, 1988), 36.

2. The Uses and Abuses of Call Outs

35   *"Movement building isn't about":* Alicia Garza, *The Purpose of Power:
        How We Come Together When We Fall Apart* (New York: One World,
        2020), 136.

38   *Instead of developing:* Elizabeth (Betita) Martinez Oral History,
        August 6, 2006, p. 30, Smith College Archives, https://compass.five
        colleges.edu/object/smith:1342641.

39   *Feminist writer Jo Freeman:* Jo (Joreen) Freeman, "TRASHING:
        The Dark Side of Sisterhood," https://www.jofreeman.com/joreen
        /trashing.htm, originally published as "Trashed: The Dark Side of
        Sisterhood," *Ms.*, April 1976, 49–51, 92–98.

39   *Even President Jimmy Carter:* Jack Eisen, "President Backs D.C.
        Vote on Hill, Carter Backs D.C. Congressional Vote," *Washington
        Post*, February 17, 1977, https://www.washingtonpost.com/archive
        /politics/1977/02/17/president-backs-dc-vote-on-hill/0f3e2bbc-7f49
        -4e40-8b3f-0cc16524f7fb/.

39   *Instead, it aggressively:* Michael Isikoff and Eric Pianin, "Lopsided
        House Vote Overturns District's Sexual Reform Law," *Washington
        Post,* October 2, 1981, https://www.washingtonpost.com/archive
        /politics/1981/10/02/lopsided-house-vote-overturns-districts-sexual
        -reform-law/5e364083-c1bb-46fa-a9f5-69b8bcfe6b37/.

41   *"speak so that you can speak again":* Zora Neale Hurston, "Mother
        Catherine" (1934), quoted in Lucy Hurston, *Speak, So You Can Speak
        Again: The Life of Zora Neale Hurston* (New York: HarperCollins,
        2004).

42   *As author Ta-Nehisi Coates:* Ta-Nehisi Coates, "The Cancella-
        tion of Colin Kaepernick," *New York Times*, November 22, 2019,
        https://www.nytimes.com/2019/11/22/opinion/colin-kaepernick
        -nfl.html.

43   *They'll criticize human:* Nardos Haile, "We Need to Talk about
        Jennifer Aniston's Misguided Take on Cancel Culture," *Salon*,
        August 23, 2023, https://www.salon.com/2023/08/23/jennifer
        -aniston-cancel-culture/.

45   *It doesn't help:* Mikael Good and Philip Wallach, "The Emotive Presi-
     dency," *National Affairs*, no. 56 (Summer 2023), https://national
     affairs.com/publications/detail/the-emotive-presidency.

46   *In response to this:* Ernest Owens, *The Case for Cancel Culture: How
     This Democratic Tool Works to Liberate Us All* (New York: St. Martin's
     Press, 2023).

46   *Most often, we:* Molly Schwartz, "Roxane Gay Says Cancel Culture
     Does Not Exist," *Mother Jones Recharge*, March 5, 2021, https://www
     .motherjones.com/media/2021/03/roxane-gay-says-cancel-culture
     -does-not-exist/.

47   *Life appears to:* Shivani Dubey, "What PR Agents and Branding
     Experts Have to Say about Cancel Culture," *HuffPost*, November 9,
     2023, https://www.huffpost.com/entry/cancel-culture-pr-branding
     _n_6545210ee4b01b2585839161.

48   *In an atmosphere:* This term has been bandied about since the 1930s
     but was particularly attached to Senator Joseph McCarthy and his
     infamous anti-Communist witch hunt in the 1950s; to decry the
     campaign against the 1987 Supreme Court nomination of Robert
     Bork; to defend President Bill Clinton during his impeachment in
     1998; and, more recently, to defend Brett Kavanaugh during his
     nomination to the Supreme Court in 2018.

49   *And as millennial:* Malikia Johnson, "Cast Down Cancel Culture:
     Elitism in Millennial Social Justice Movements," *Grassroots Economic
     Organizing*, September 25, 2017, https://geo.coop/story/cast-down
     -cancel-culture.

50   *Natalie Wynn, a:* Natalie Wynn, "Canceling," ContraPoints, educa-
     tional video, 1:31:48, January 2, 2020, https://www.youtube.com
     /watch?v=OjMPJVmXxV8.

55   *"Whatever begins in":* Benjamin Franklin, *Poor Richard's Almanack,
     1734: An Almanack for the Year of Christ 1734* (Philadelphia: New
     Printing-Office near the Market; Yale University Library).

56   *"We then tear":* adrienne maree brown, *We Will Not Cancel Us*
     (Chico, CA: AK Press, 2020), 66.

57   *As columnist David:* David Brooks, "The Cruelty of Call Out Cul-
     ture," *New York Times*, January 14, 2019, https://www.nytimes.com
     /2019/01/14/opinion/call-out-social-justice.html.

57   *Given that 64 percent:* Centers for Disease Control and Prevention,
     "Fast Facts: Preventing Adverse Childhood Experiences," National
     Center for Injury Prevention and Control, Division of Violence

Prevention, June 29, 2023, https://www.cdc.gov/violenceprevention /aces/fastfact.html.

57   *As Ana Marie Cox:* Ana Marie Cox, "We Are Not Just Polarized. We Are *Traumatized,*" *New Republic*, September 14, 2023, https:// newrepublic.com/article/175311/america-polarized-traumatized -trump-violence.

57   *Black feminist Flo:* Gloria Steinem, "The Verbal Karate of Florynce R. Kennedy, Esq.," *Ms.*, August 19, 2011, https://msmagazine.com /2011/08/19/the-verbal-karate-of-florynce-r-kennedy-esq/. Confirmed in personal conversation with Gloria Steinem, May 12, 2023.

58   *As writer Cherríe:* Cherríe Moraga, "La Güera," in *This Bridge Called My Back: Writings by Radical Women of Color*, 4th ed. (New York: State University of New York Press, 2015), 22–29.

58   *"Whereas harm is a":* Da'Shaun Harrison, "Committing Harm Is Not the Same as Being Abusive," *Intersectional Feminist Media*, February 11, 2020, https://wyvarchive.com/abuse-harm-disposability-politics.

59   *AIDS historian and:* Sarah Schulman, *Conflict Is Not Abuse: Overstating Harm, Community Responsibility, and the Duty of Repair* (Vancouver, Canada: Arsenal Pulp Press, 2016), 21.

60   *Sometimes a calling:* Paulo Freire, *Pedagogy of the Oppressed* (New York: Continuum Press, 2007), 44.

61   *Look, for instance:* Kevin Breuninger, "New *Teen Vogue* Editor-in-Chief Alexi McCammond Resigns Over Past Racist Tweets About Asians," CNC.com, March 19, 2021, https://www.cnbc.com /2021/03/18/teen-vogue-editor-in-chief-alexi-mccammond-resigns -over-old-tweet-firestorm.html.

62   *By the end of:* Dani Di Placido, "The Ballad of 'Bean Dad' Shows the Cruel, Petty Side of Twitter," *Forbes*, January 5, 2021, https:// www.forbes.com/sites/danidiplacido/2021/01/05/the-ballad-of -bean-dad-shows-the-cruel-petty-side-of-twitter/; also, Michael Rietmulder, *Seattle Times,* January 5, 2021, https://www.seattletimes .com/entertainment/music/seattles-john-roderick-aka-bean-dad -apologizes-after-social-media-backlash/.

64   *As poet June:* June Jordan, "Do You Do Well to be Angry?" *Progressive Magazine*, November 2, 2001, https://progressive.org/magazine/well-angry/.

64   *After all, as journalist:* Bonny Brooks, "How Contemporary Capitalism Drives Hysterical Wokeness," *Medium*, August 14, 2018, https:// medium.com/arc-digital/how-contemporary-capitalism-drives -hysterical-wokeness-9fb206158aad.

67   *In his reporting on:* Conor Friedersdorf, "The Destructiveness of Call-Out Culture on Campus," *Atlantic*, May 8, 2017, https://www .theatlantic.com/politics/archive/2017/05/call-out-culture-is-stressing -out-college-students/524679/.

67   *After the controversy at:* Susan Svrluga, "After Turmoil, Harvard Students Return to a Changed Campus," *Washington Post*, February 4, 2024, https://www.washingtonpost.com/education/2024/02 /04/harvard-students-return-turmoil-aftermath.

68   *Language policing is:* Keith Humphreys, "The Burden of Proof Is on the Language Police," *Atlantic Magazine*, August 7, 2023, https:// www.theatlantic.com/ideas/archive/2023/08/addiction-drug-policy -language-harm-evidence/674907.

68   *"There is an underlying":* Frances Lee, "Excommunicate Me from the Church of Social Justice," *Autostraddle,* July 13, 2017, https://www .autostraddle.com/kin-aesthetics-excommunicate-me-from-the -church-of-social-justice-386640/.

69   *One of my students:* Rebecca Alvara, "Coalition Building Through Calling In: A Necessary Step for Change," student essay, Fall 2020, Smith College.

69   *"calling out causes people to think about their reputations":* Margot Audero, personal communication to author, May 20, 2024.

70   *As* Everyday Feminism *writer:* Hari Ziyad, "6 Ways to Tell If You Need to be Called Out," *Everyday Feminism*, May 31, 2016, https:// everydayfeminism.com/2016/05/when-calling-out-is-necessary/.

70   *"Constructive kindness is":* Walter Rhein, "How Constructive Kindness Is More Effective Than Constant Criticism," *Medium*, January 19, 2024, https://medium.com/thirty-over-fifty/how-constructive -kindness-is-more-effective-than-constant-criticism-cea75b6fe510.

72   *She argued that:* Audre Lorde, "The Uses of Anger," Speech to the National Women's Studies Association, 1981, *Women's Studies Quarterly* 9, no. 3 (Fall 1981): 7–10.

3. Be Strategic

73   *"A new type of thinking":* Albert Einstein, telegram quoted in the *New York Times*, May 25, 1946, https://www.nytimes.com/1946/05 /25/archives/atomic-education-urged-by-einstein-scientist-in -plea-for-200000-to.html.

77   *Later that week:* Alexandra Minna Stern, "Forced Sterilization Policies in the US Targeted Minorities and Those with Disabilities—

and Lasted into the 21st Century," *The Conversation*, Michigan Institute for Health Policy and Innovation, August 26, 2020, https://theconversation.com/forced-sterilization-policies-in-the-us-targeted-minorities-and-those-with-disabilities-and-lasted-into-the-21st-century-143144.

77 *Voting rights activist:* Sanjana Manjeshwar, "America's Forgotten History of Forced Sterilization," *Berkeley Political Review*, November 4, 2020, https://bpr.berkeley.edu/2020/11/04/americas-forgotten-history-of-forced-sterilization/.

79 *And as Fan Xuan Chen:* Diana Yates, "Vigilantism Is an Identity for Some People, Researchers Report," University of Illinois Urbana-Champaign, March 10, 2022, https://news.illinois.edu/view/6367/1322325276.

80 *We should remember:* Maurice Mitchell, "Building Resilient Organizations," *Forge*, November 29, 2022, https://forgeorganizing.org/article/building-resilient-organizations.

80 *We should seek to:* Lea E. Williams, "Making a Life, Not Making a Living: The Servant Leadership of Ella Josephine Baker," *Servants of the People: The 1960s Legacy of African American Leadership*, 2nd ed. (New York: Palgrave Macmillan, 2009), 163–81.

82 *As the late congresswoman:* Barbara Jordan, Commencement Address, Harvard University, 1977, cited in https://txwf.org/barbara-jordan-a-voice-for-democracy/.

86 *The ecologist had a good:* Zenobia Jeffries Warfield, "The World Is a Miraculous Mess, and It's Going to Be All Right," interview with adrienne maree brown, *Yes!*, March 27, 2018, https://www.yesmagazine.org/social-justice/2018/03/27/the-world-is-a-miraculous-mess-and-its-going-to-be-alright.

88 *Journalist Amanda Ripley explains:* Amanda Ripley, "Why We Split the World into Good and Evil and Make Decisions that We Regret," *Washington Post*, January 4, 2024, https://www.washingtonpost.com/opinions/2024/01/04/hamas-israel-good-evil-splitting-amanda-ripley/.

92 *Some will see themselves:* Eve Fairbanks, "The Reasonable Rebels," *Washington Post*, August 29, 2019, https://www.washingtonpost.com/outlook/2019/08/29/conservatives-say-weve-abandoned-reason-civility-old-south-said-that-too/?arc404=true.

92 *Scholar-activist Keeanga-Yamahtta:* Keeanga-Yamahtta Taylor, "Don't Shame the First Steps of the Resistance," SocialistWorker.org, Janu-

ary 24, 2017, https://socialistworker.org/2017/01/24/dont-shame
-the-first-steps-of-a-resistance.

92   *We have to embrace*: Kelly Hayes and Mariame Kaba, "How Much
Discomfort Is the Whole World Worth?," *Boston Review*, September 6, 2023, https://www.bostonreview.net/articles/how-much
-discomfort-is-the-whole-world-worth.

94   *According to the Movement*: Movement for Black Lives, "Perspectives
on Community Safety from Black America," December 5, 2023,
https://m4bl.org/wp-content/uploads/2023/12/Perspectives
-on-Community-Safety-From-Black-America.pdf.

95   *As Audre Lorde said*: Audre Lorde, *Sister Outsider: Essays and
Speeches* (New York: Ten Speed Press, 1984), 77.

96   *When asked by a reporter*: Adrienne T. Washington, "A Bad First
Date with Mr. Obama," *Washington Times*, February 1, 2009, https://
www.washingtontimes.com/news/2009/feb/1/a-bad-first-date-with
-mr-obama/.

97   *Our surprising unity*: For a fuller discussion, see Jael Silliman, Marlene Gerber Fried, Loretta Ross, and Elena R. Gutiérrez, *Undivided
Rights: Women of Color Organize for Reproductive Justice*, 2nd ed.
(Chicago: Haymarket Books, 2004).

4. Model the World We Desire

105   *"There can be no"*: Justin Lee, "White Nationalism's Therapeutics
of Hate," *Medium*, May 11, 2018, https://medium.com/arc-digital
/white-nationalisms-therapeutics-of-hate-ecb1bc1731ea.

114   *He organized the first*: Rev. C. T. Vivian and Steve Fiffer, *It's in the
Action: Memories of a Nonviolent Warrior* (Montgomery, AL: New
South Books, 2021), 21. (Published posthumously.)

117   *In my Appropriate Whiteness*: Sonya Renee Taylor, *The Body Is Not
An Apology: The Power of Radical Self-Love* (Oakland, CA: Berrett-
Koehler Publishers, 2018), 17.

117   *Whereas guilt is*: Kai Cheng Thom, "9 Ways to Be Accountable When
You've Been Abusive," *Everyday Feminism*, February 1, 2016, https://
everydayfeminism.com/2016/02/be-accountable-when-abusive/.

118   *For example, when two*: "Black Men Arrested at Philadelphia Star-
bucks Feared for Their Lives," *Guardian*, April 19, 2018, https://
www.theguardian.com/business/2018/apr/19/starbucks-black-men
-feared-for-lives-philadelphia.

118 *Young voters were the:* "How Groups Voted in 2020," Roper Center, https://ropercenter.cornell.edu/how-groups-voted-2020; "National Exit Poll for Presidential Results," CBS News, December 14, 2020, https://www.cbsnews.com/elections/2020/united-states/president/exit-poll/.

119 *Psychologist Adam Grant has said:* Nick Hobson, "Adam Grant Says the Key to Lifelong Learning Comes Down to This 1 Thing. You Might Not Like It," *Inc.*, May 24, 2024, https://www.inc.com/nick-hobson/adam-grant-says-key-to-lifelong-learning-comes-down-to-this-1-thing-you-might-not-like-it.html.

121 *"Kindness is a language":* The Center for Mark Twain Studies reports that although this quote is frequently attributed to Twain, there is no evidence that he originally said that. https://marktwainstudies.com/apocryphaltwainoptimism/.

122 *Sociologist Noël A. Cazenave:* Kimberly Phillips, "Not Random: UConn Researcher Looks at Kindness as Deliberate Way to Affect Change," *UConn Today*, August 9, 2023, https://today.uconn.edu/2023/08/not-random-uconn-researcher-looks-at-kindness-as-deliberate-way-to-affect-change.

122 *Feminist philosopher Virginia Held:* Virginia Held, *The Ethics of Care: Personal, Political, and Global*, 2nd ed. (New York: Oxford University Press, 2006), 10.

122 *empathy is a skill:* Jamil Zaki, *The War for Kindness: Building Empathy in a Fractured World* (New York: Crown Books, 2019), 13.

122 *Writer David Brooks reported:* David Brooks, "How America Got Mean," *Atlantic*, August 14, 2023, https://www.theatlantic.com/magazine/archive/2023/09/us-culture-moral-education-formation/674765/.

123 *When we set our moral:* Viktor Frankl, *Man's Search for Meaning* (New York: Pocket, 1959), 76.

123 *Maya Angelou advised:* Maya Angelou, "'We need joy as we need air. We need love as we need water. We need each other as we need the earth we share.' #MayaAngelou Happy Earth Day!" Facebook post, April 22, 2022, https://www.facebook.com/MayaAngelou/posts/we-need-joy-as-we-need-air-we-need-love-as-we-need-water-we-need-each-other-as-w/10161023526344796/.

124 *She advises that to:* adrienne maree brown, *Pleasure Activism* (Chico, CA: AK Press, 2019), 13–14.

124 *Black feminist writer:* Kay Bonetti, "Interview with Toni Cade Bam-

bara," American Audio Prose Library, 1982, https://searchworks
.stanford.edu/view/3262851.

125   *As civil rights activist Rev. William Barber said:* Jack Jenkins, "'You Wear Out': How Chronic Illness Grounds and Inspires William Barber's Activism," *United Methodist Insight,* June 22, 2022, https:// um-insight.net/in-the-world/advocating-justice/you-wear-out-how -chronic-illness-grounds-and-inspires-willia/

128   *"To be hopeful in bad":* Howard Zinn, "The Optimism of Uncertainty," *Nation,* September 2, 2004, https://www.thenation.com /article/politics/optimism-uncertainty/.

132   *In it, King spoke:* Martin Luther King Jr., "Remaining Awake Through a Great Revolution," Speech, National Cathedral, Washington, DC, March 31, 1968, Congressional Record 114, no. 7 (April 9, 1968): 58–64, https://www.congress.gov/bound-congressional-record/1968 /04/09/extensions-of-remarks-section?p=1.

132   *And yet, King said:* King, "Remaining Awake."

133   *King argued that:* King, "Remaining Awake."

133   *King stated:* King, "Remaining Awake."

135   *As Civil Rights scholar:* Marian Wright Edelman, "Dr. Vincent Harding's Call to Make America America," *HuffPost,* May 30, 2014, https:// www.huffpost.com/entry/dr-vincent-hardings-call_b_5420254.

135   *As Audre Lorde said:* Audre Lorde, *A Burst of Light* (Ithaca, NY: Firebrand, 1988), 42.

137   *We can build a:* Merle Woo, "Letter to Ma," in *This Bridge Called My Back: Writings by Radical Women of Color,* eds. Cherríe Moraga and Gloria E. Anzaldúa (Berkeley, CA: Third Woman Press, 1981), 221.

137   *As Rev. angel Kyodo:* Rev. angel Kyodo williams, "The World Is Our Field of Practice," *On Being with Kristina Tippett,* April 19, 2018, https://onbeing.org/programs/angel-kyodo-williams-the-world-is -our-field-of-practice/.

5. Starting with the Self

139   *"Love is that condition":* Maya Angelou, interview by Oprah Winfrey, *Super Soul Sunday,* OWN, May 19, 2013, https://www.youtube.com /watch?v=Irs5tJgokys.

143   *Since then, my hard:* Audre Lorde, "The Uses of Anger: Women Responding to Racism," *Sister Outsider: Essays and Speeches,* rev. ed. (1984; Berkeley, CA: Crossing Press, 2007), 124–33.

144 *As embodiment facilitator:* Samhita Mukhopadhyay, "Doing the Work While Doing the Work," *Nation*, July 11, 2023, https://www.thenation.com/article/society/social-justice-trauma-healing/.

144 *As Martin Luther King Jr.:* Dr. Martin Luther King Jr., *Where Do We Go from Here: Chaos or Community?* (1967; repr., New York: Beacon Press, 2010), 43.

145 *In "Notes of a Native Son":* James Baldwin, "Notes of a Native Son," *Notes of a Native Son* (Boston: Beacon Press, 1955), 101.

146 *Psychologist Thomas Curran observes:* Thomas Curran, *The Perfection Trap: Embracing the Power of Good Enough* (New York: Scribner, 2023), 40.

148 *In* Eloquent Rage: Brittney Cooper, *Eloquent Rage: A Black Feminist Discovers Her Superpower* (New York: St. Martin's Press, 2018), 204.

149 *As adrienne maree brown:* adrienne maree brown, "attention liberation: a commitment, a year of practice," *adrienne maree brown* (blog), January 1, 2018 https://adriennemareebrown.net/2018/01/01/attention-liberation-a-commitment-a-year-of-practice/.

6. Calling In Techniques

155 *In recognizing the humanity:* "Thurgood Marshall," Biography, updated January 11, 2021, https://www.biography.com/legal-figures/thurgood-marshall.

156 *As neuropsychology professor:* Arthur Bloch, *Murphy's Law Book Two: More Reasons Why Things Go Wrong* (New Rochelle, NY: Magnum, 1981), 52.

156 *Sure, you could challenge:* Walter Rhein, "All Bigotry Is Ignorance, But Not All Ignorance Is Bigotry," *Medium*, November 2, 2023, https://medium.com/our-human-family/all-bigotry-is-ignorance-but-not-all-ignorance-is-bigotry-ef0a181f112d.

162 *People are complicated:* Leoni Jesner and Rufus Toney Spann, "What Are Control Issues? Causes, Signs and Treatments," *Forbes Health*, March 13, 2023, https://www.forbes.com/health/mind/what-are-control-issues/.

172 *Scholar and activist:* Fania E. Davis, *The Little Book of Race and Restorative Justice*, (New York: Good Books, 2019), 14.

172 *It seeks to find forgiveness:* Davis, *The Little Book of Race and Restorative Justice*, 28.

7. Creating a Call In Culture

177 *"I may be wrong and"*: Karl Popper, *The Myth of the Framework: In Defence of Science and Rationality* ed. M. A. Notturno, (New York: Routledge Press, 1994), xii.

180 *As political theorist:* Mie Inouye, "Solidarity Now," *Boston Review*, September 19, 2023, https://www.bostonreview.net/forum/solidarity -now/.

182 *There is no consensus*: Inouye, "Solidarity Now."

182 *"spearpoint" words:* Katherine Cross, *Log Off: Why Posting and Politics (Almost) Never Mix*, (New York: LittlePuss Press, 2024).

187 *Another model I love:* Annaliese Griffin, "Three Words You Need for Your Next Hard Conversation," *Medium*, August 10, 2020, https:// forge.medium.com/three-words-you-need-for-your-next-hard -conversation-a3e2090d043d.

188 *Re-expression puts a few extra steps:* Kerry Patterson, Joseph Grenny, Ron McMillan, and Al Switzler, *Crucial Conversations: Tools for Talking When Stakes are High*, 2nd ed. (New York: McGraw Hill, 2012), 171.

190 *"We currently live in a reality"*: Zenobia Jeffries Warfield, "The World Is a Miraculous Mess, and It's Going to Be All Right: Interview with adrienne maree brown," *Yes!* magazine, March 27, 2018, https:// www.yesmagazine.org/social-justice/2018/03/27/the-world-is-a -miraculous-mess-and-its-going-to-be-alright.

191 *The goal is not:* Michael S. Roth, *Safe Enough Spaces: A Pragmatist's Approach to Inclusion, Free Speech, and Political Correctness on College Campuses* (New Haven, CT: Yale University Press, 2019), 101.

192 *Leaders can even try:* Mary Rowe, "Micro-inequities (Including Micro-aggressions) and Micro-affirmations," MIT Sloan School of Management, faculty page, https://mitmgmtfaculty.mit.edu/mrowe /micro-inequities/.

194 *But if you're just anxious:* Ossiana Tepfenhart, "'Nazis Are Very Nice, Polite People,' She Said," *Medium*, July 20, 2023, https://medium .com/@ossiana.tepfenhart/nazis-are-very-nice-polite-people-she -said-b1f76aa8694e.

196 *After Trump's 2016 victory:* Joe Pinsker, "Trump's Presidency Is Over. So Are Many Relationships," *Atlantic*, March 30, 2021, https://www .theatlantic.com/family/archive/2021/03/trump-friend-family -relationships/618457/.

204 *The students in my classes:* Dashka Slater, "Authors Like Me Are Fighting the Book-Ban Zealots. We Need Help," *Mother Jones*, September–October 2023, https://www.motherjones.com/politics /2023/08/mothers-liberty-book-bans-republican-ron-desantis -culture-wars-censorship/.

204 *After swastikas were found:* Ben James, "In Smith Swastika Incident, One Professor Asks, '"Can We Stay Focused on the Fascists?'" New England Public Radio, November 27, 2019, https://www.nepm.org /regional-news/2019-11-27/in-smith-swastika-incident-one -professor-asks-can-we-stay-focused-on-the-fascists.

208 *"calls for greater freedom":* Richard Amesbury and Catherine O'Donnell, "Dear Administrators: Enough With the Free-Speech Rhetoric!," *Chronicle of Higher Education*, November 16, 2023, https:// www.chronicle.com/article/dear-administrators-enough-with-the -free-speech-rhetoric.

210 *University of Pennsylvania campus:* Sigal R Ben-Porath, *Cancel Wars: How Universities Can Foster Free Speech, Promote Inclusion, and Renew Democracy* (Chicago: University of Chicago Press, 2023), 1, 46.

8. Redemption After a Call In

215 *"We all fuck up":* Ngọc Loan Trần, "Calling In: A Less Disposable Way of Holding Each Other Accountable," December 13, 2013, *BGD Blog*, https://www.bgdblog.org/2013/12/calling-less-disposable -way-holding-accountable/.

216 *And two years before:* Rainey Horwitz, "The Dalkon Shield," The Embryo Project Encyclopedia, January 10, 2018, https://embryo.asu .edu/pages/dalkon-shield.

217 *She'd become vice:* Yulanda Ward, "Spatial Deconcentration in DC: US Housing Policy After the Urban Rebellions of the 1960s," October 9, 2019 (reprinted posthumously), https://notesfrom below.org/article/spatial-deconcentration-dc; see also: Al Kamen and Benjamin Weiser, "3 SE Men Plead Guilty to Murder of Housing Activist," *Washington Post*, November 16, 1981, https://www .washingtonpost.com/archive/local/1981/11/17/3-se-men-plead -guilty-to-murder-of-housing-activist/530f8f37-4bc2-4b9b-98d6 -23be95d312be/.

220 *There is a strength:* Bryan Stevenson, *Just Mercy: A Story of Justice and Redemption* (New York: Spiegel & Grau, 2014), 290.

222 *As Chris Singleton:* Rasha Ali, "Five Years After Charleston Church Massacre: How 'Emmanuel' Reveals the Power of Forgiveness," *USA Today,* June 17, 2019, https://www.usatoday.com/story/life/movies /2019/06/17/emanuel-explores-power-forgiveness-after-charleston -church-massacre/1478473001/.

224 *"Finding the truth in":* Walter Rhein, "All Bigotry Is Ignorance, But Not All Ignorance Is Bigotry," *Medium*, November 2, 2023, https:// medium.com/our-human-family/all-bigotry-is-ignorance-but-not -all-ignorance-is-bigotry-ef0a181f112d.

229 *"True accountability is not only apologizing":* Mia Mingus, "Four Parts to Accountability," Leaving Evidence, December 18, 2019, https://leavingevidence.wordpress.com/2019/12/18/how-to-give-a -good-apology-part-1-the-four-parts-of-accountability/

Epilogue

237 *"Don't ask what the world":* Brittini L. Palmer, The Key to Howard Thurman's Spirituality Is 'What Makes You Come Alive,'" *Sojourners*, March 14, 2023, https://sojo.net/articles/key-howard-thurman-s -spirituality-what-makes-you-come-alive.

237 *Dr. King said:* Murray Schumach, "Martin Luther King Jr.'s Original *New York Times* Obituary," January 18, 2021 (originally published April 5, 1968), *New York Times*, https://www.nytimes.com/article /martin-luther-king-jr.html.

INDEX

Index

Index

Index

Index

Index

Index

Index

Index

Index

Index

ABOUT THE AUTHOR

LORETTA J. ROSS is an activist, professor, and public intellectual. In her five decades in the human rights movement, she's deprogrammed white supremacists, taught convicted rapists the principles of feminism, and organized the second-largest march on Washington (surpassed only by the 2017 Women's March). A cofounder of the National Center for Human Rights Education and the SisterSong Women of Color Reproductive Justice Collective, her many accolades and honors include a 2022 MacArthur Fellowship and a 2024 induction into the National Women's Hall of Fame. Today, Ross is an associate professor at Smith College in Northampton, Massachusetts, and a partner with the consulting firm 14th Strategies, with which she runs calling in training sessions at organizations around the country.

ABOUT THE TYPE

This book was set in Avenir and Minion Pro. Avenir is a sans serif typeface designed by Adrian Frutiger in 1988. It has a clean, modern approach to design, making it versatile and widely used in branding, signage, and editorial design. Minion Pro is a serif typeface designed by Robert Slimbach and released by Adobe in 1990. Inspired by Renaissance typefaces, it's known for its traditional appearance. Minion Pro offers a versatile range of weights and styles.